MODERN WORLD NATIONS

MODERN WORLD NATIONS

South
Korea

Christopher L. Salter
University of Missouri, Columbia

Series Consulting Editor
Charles F. Gritzner
South Dakota State University

CHELSEA HOUSE
PUBLISHERS
A Haights Cross Communications Company

Philadelphia

Frontispiece: Flag of South Korea

Cover: Haein-sa Temple.

Dedicated to Sweet Chloe and Breakfast Creek

CHELSEA HOUSE PUBLISHERS

VP, NEW PRODUCT DEVELOPMENT Sally Cheney
DIRECTOR OF PRODUCTION Kim Shinners
CREATIVE MANAGER Takeshi Takahashi
MANUFACTURING MANAGER Diann Grasse

Staff for SOUTH KOREA

EDITOR Lee Marcott
PRODUCTION EDITOR Noelle Nardone
PICTURE RESEARCHER Sarah Bloom
SERIES DESIGNER Takeshi Takahashi
COVER DESIGNER Keith Trego
LAYOUT 21st Century Publishing and Communications, Inc.

A Haights Cross Communications ✦ Company ®

www.chelseahouse.com

3 5 7 9 8 6 4 2

Library of Congress Cataloging-in-Publication Data

Salter, Christopher L.
   South Korea / C. L. Salter.
      p. cm.—(Modern world nations)
Contents: Introduction—South Korean natural landscapes—South Korean historical
geography—South Korean people and culture—South Korean government—The economy
of South Korea—Contemporary South Korean regional identities—The future of South Korea.
   ISBN 0-7910-8662-3
   1. Korea (South) [1. Korea (South)] I. Title. II. Series.
DS902 .S258 2002
951.95—dc21

                                                                    2002012361

Table of Contents

South Korea

Seoul is the capital of South Korea. This early morning view of the city shows the buildings that house the people as well as the government, commercial, and cultural institutions of the country.

1

Introduction: The Power of Geographic Location

The Korean Peninsula is an extension of the Asian continent. When both North and South Korea are combined, the total area is slightly larger than the state of Utah. It is in a most delicate location, for to the northwest lies the enormous country of China; and to the far northeast the Korean Peninsula borders the even larger Russia. To the east lies the island world of Japan and while it is not a particularly large country, it has an economic and cultural dominance that the Korean world has had to deal with for more than 2,000 years. South and North Korea make up a world that is truly shaped by location.

This peninsula—just as in the case of the two countries of North and South Korea now—has had its origins and history continually influenced by the proximity of China lying just to the north and the west. Chinese settlers, for nearly 2,500 years, have had interest in the alluvial valley of the Yalu River that serves as the border between the peninsula and the Chinese Northeast, or what the West has known as Manchuria. As early as the Chinese Shang dynasty (ca. 1726–1122 B.C.) there are records of Chinese settlers occupying the river valley of the Taedong River where the North Korean capital of Pyongyang is today.

From another direction came early migration from the northern Japanese island of Hokkaido. This brought Ainu people from Japan to the southern Korean Peninsula. And although there is no record of early migration from Russia in the peopling of the Korean Peninsula, the current history of both North and South Korea shows strong influences from the Russian world as well as a continuing Chinese and Japanese force.

The Korean Peninsula has been known by two names to the Western world. Traditionally it was the "Land of the Morning Calm." Lying at the eastern edge of the world's largest continent, and at the doorway of the giant China, this name shows the Korean pride in being the stable, productive, and creative country that got the early sun as it rose over Japan and worked its way toward China and the world further west.

But it is also known as the "Hermit Kingdom." Having had so much of the peninsula's history influenced, perhaps confused, by the continual cultural shifts caused by Chinese and, later, Japanese, and then Western countries either seeking space on the peninsula, or using the long narrow geography of Korea as a pathway for military or mercantile ambitions, the peninsula was closed almost completely from the early 1600s until the last quarter of the 1800s. The Hermit Kingdom, as a name, reflected the Korean wish to not have to deal with contesting foreign religions, economic systems, and governmental authorities. From 1640 until

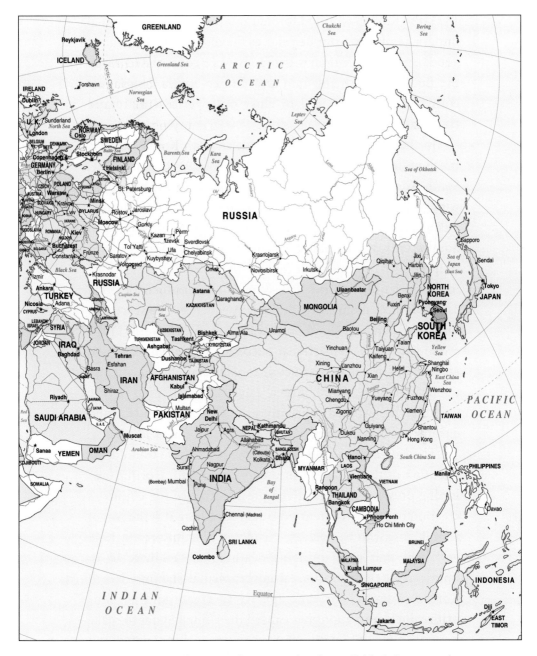

Although historically one nation, Korea has been divided since 1945 between a Communist north and a non-Communist south. Both are considered part of East Asia, which also includes China, Taiwan, Japan, Macao, and the numerous islands near their shores.

1873, the Koreans limited foreign interaction to "the annual imperial embassy from Beijing" as the only legal exchange of goods and ideas. Wooden palisades were constructed along the flood plains of the Yalu and Tumen Rivers (northwest corner of the peninsula) to close out overland mainland traffic as completely as possible.

In the Korean world of the 21st century, North Korea is much more inclined to play the hermit role. At the same time, South Korea gives great energy to expanding its interaction with global markets and international economic and cultural linkages. Hosting the 1988 Olympics at Seoul, the capital of South Korea, was a bold representation of the country's wish to no longer be seen as simply another "developing nation" in the cluster of countries that seemed to be classified too often as of minor economic or cultural consequence. The success in the 1988 Olympic Games opened the eyes of the world to the economic and organizational successes of South Korea. In architecture, urban infrastructure, organizational capacity, and political stability, South Korea caught the attention of the world. It has worked diligently ever since to maintain and enhance such a changing perception.

The Korean Peninsula's capacity to continue to hold the attention of the broader world continues. With North Korea having only its second official president since the country's creation in 1948—current president Kim Jong Il is the son of Kim Il Sung who was declared leader of North Korea in 1948 and held that post until his death in 1994—there is an impressive demonstration of governmental stability. North Korea's potential for the capacity to create and perhaps utilize nuclear weapons has caused the United States to make a number of diplomatic efforts to rein in this isolated and little-known country.

South Korea's strong economic growth during the final two decades of the 20th century until the 1997 Asian financial crisis (in 1998 the South Korean economy *shrunk* more than

South Koreans searched job listings posted at the Seoul railway station as part of a campaign by social workers to help those unemployed during the economic crisis of the late 1990s.

7 percent after having *grown* an average of more than 7 percent annually for the prior decade) had established the country as one of the so-called Asian Tigers (or some say "dragons") in economic success and development.

While the 1997 so-called Asian Flu that began in Thailand spread all through insular and peninsular Southeast Asia—as well as China, Taiwan, and Japan—South Korea was unusually effective in rebounding from this regional economic slow-down. By the late 1990s, South Korea had not only repaid all of the $57 billion that the International Monetary Fund had loaned the country, but it had also turned its economy around and was again making major strides toward economic leadership in East Asia. So while one of the two Koreas was only tentatively opening its doors and consciousness to the broader world, the other Korea was striding full speed ahead toward a more aggressive role in East Asian and world economic affairs.

The Korean Peninsula has another unusual trait to reflect upon when considering South Korea. Even though the geographic location of the peninsula jutting out from East Asia into the Sea of Japan has caused it to be used as a stepping-stone toward Japan, or from Japan toward the Asian continent, the ethnic composition of the two countries is almost completely Korean. Korean stock is composed of the Altaic family of races, which includes the Turkish, Mongolian, and Tungusic peoples.

Contemporary population in South Korea is 99.9 percent Korean, while North Korea is just a fraction less homogeneous, being 99.8 percent Korean. The Chinese make up some 0.2 percent of the population in the North, while a very small population of other migrant peoples make up the 0.1 percent "other" population of South Korea. This compares to a China that is only 92 percent ethnically Han Chinese, or with a Japan that is 99.1 percent Japanese.

From numbers like these it can be seen that the Korean Peninsula has been a geographic corridor to further destinations for migrants and military, but has not generally served actively as a primary target destination for either sojourners or permanent migrants seeking new beginnings or creating new settlements.

And what is the future for a peninsula that is now entering its sixth decade as a divided landscape? What lessons can be learned from studying the personalities of South Korea and, later in contrast, of North Korea? What political and economic facts help explain such divergent patterns of recent development between the two Koreas, especially when compared to the nearly seamless development of the whole peninsula for the past 2,500 years?

The search for the answers to such questions begins by considering the features of the geographic personality and identity of South Korea.

These fields in Chorwon, South Korea, fall just below the 38th parallel, which is the dividing line between North and South Korea.

2

South Korean Natural Landscapes

AREA AND LANDFORMS

S outh Korea has an area of 38,402 square miles (99,461 square kilometers). It is the southern part of the Korean Peninsula, which juts off the eastern edge of the continent of Asia. It is divided from North Korea along the 38th parallel of latitude. This is a somewhat arbitrary—that is, political rather than physical geographic—dividing line determined at the end of World War II. It became apparent to the West that the Soviet Union's entrance into the Pacific theater at the very end of World War II was opportunistic. It was done more for national gain than symbolic cooperation with the Allied forces fighting against the Japanese in East and Southeast Asia. It then became essential to split the Korean Peninsula into two realms. The Soviets controlled the northern one. The United States controlled the southern one.

The 38th parallel had some precedent as a partition, and it did have some geographic features that supported it as a dividing line for 55 percent (north) and 45 percent (south) of the peninsula. Mineral wealth was more abundant in the north, and agricultural land was much better in the south. And, most logically, what came to be North Korea shared a short border with the U.S.S.R. and its new ally, the People's Republic of China. This 1948 division has been the de facto border between the two Koreas for more than half a century.

South Korea has the Yellow Sea and the East China Sea on the west and south. On the eastern side lies the Sea of Japan. There are some 3,000 islands that are seen as part of the two countries of the peninsula, although most of them are uninhabited. The largest of all the Korean islands is Cheju Island, an integral part of South Korea. It lies to the south, southwest of South Korea, and has an area of 713 square miles (1,846 square kilometers), and is a province. The island has a rather unique history reflecting relative independence from the rest of the peninsula.

The whole landscape of South Korea is characterized by very hilly topography, made smooth only where river valleys are cut from the Taebaek Mountains on the eastern edge of the peninsula and on the flanks of the Sobaek Mountains as they run diagonally toward the southwest border of South Korea. The Taebaek Mountains run generally from north to south, while the Sobaek are southwest to northeast in their trend. The 819 miles (1,319 kilometers) of South Korea's coastline are relatively smooth on the eastern side of the country and highly indented on the embayed western side. This has created a landscape that is characterized by small fishing villages that have long taken advantage of the resources of the Yellow Sea and its marine life. The

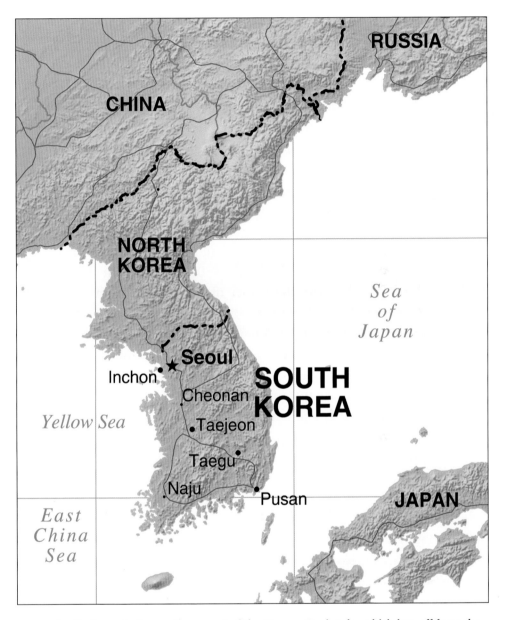

South Korea is the southern part of the Korean Peninsula, which juts off from the eastern edge of Asia. South Korea has the Yellow Sea on the west, the East China Sea on the south, and the Sea of Japan on the east. It has a very hilly topography, made smooth only where river valleys are cut from the mountains. The coastal plains and the south-facing river valleys provide the major areas for agriculture and human settlement in the country.

overall extent of South Korea is approximately 300 miles (480 kilometers) from north to south and 185 miles (298 kilometers) from east to west.

The coastal plains and the south-facing river valleys provide the major agricultural and settled landscapes of the country. One of the distinctive landscape features of this country is the high tidal range near Inchon in the Kanghwa Bay region on the western side of the peninsula. The tidal range may amount to as much as 30 feet (9 meters) along this part of the west coast while corresponding latitudes on the east coast of the peninsula will seldom have a tidal range of more than three feet (a meter). There are no natural channels that enable the South Koreans to capture the power of this daily flux in water level, but it has forced a creative wharfing and village landscape design to be able to accommodate such a daily change in water levels.

Realize that overall the Korean Peninsula is a land of mountains and substantial hill lands. While none of the peaks or the mountain systems take on the scale of similar topography in either Japan or China, there is a totality to the presence of mountains in both South and North Korea that, at least from the air, creates an impression that geographer George Cressey described as "[a land that] resembles a sea in a heavy gale." He goes on to point out, "High mountains are uncommon; it is [the mountains] profusion here that is impressive. No plain is so extensive that the encircling mountains cannot be seen on a fair day."

The broad regions of North and South Korea are separated in part by a valley that slices from the northeast to the southwest. This serves as a strong visual divide between the two sections of the peninsula as they lie segmented into South Korea and North Korea. The regional system that follows can be used to delineate distinct landscapes and land use on the entire peninsula.

REGIONS

The Korean Peninsula has six primary geographic regions. Three of these lie almost completely within the perimeter of South Korea. Getting some sense of this regional geography highlights the stage on which the drama of Korean development—both northern and southern—has taken place and will continue to take place.

The Central Mountains

The largest of the three regions in South Korea is centered on the Taebaek and Sobaek Mountain ranges. Nearly 25 percent of the South Korean population is settled in the farming villages and small towns of the Central Mountain region. The population density of the region is lightest toward the north and the east. The eastern coast has the smoother coastline and fewer fishing villages. In the uplands, there are small villages that specialize mostly in dry (rainfall) farming with some terraced rice paddy farming where water has been controlled adequately to support the traditionally more productive and favored growing of irrigated rice.

The Naktong River has its origin in the northeastern segment of this region (near Taebaek, the village that provides the name of the dominant mountain system in the Central Mountains) in the Taebaek-san (Mountains) and drains to the south southwest and finally into Ulsan Bay at the major city of Pusan. The Han River has its origin further north (above the coastal city of Kangnung) in the same mountain system. It flows south and then westward and ultimately northward. It is the major river of the capital city of Seoul (population 9.9 million) and flows into Kanghwa Bay through a significant estuary that pours into the bay north of Inchon, the fourth largest city of South Korea (population 2.5 million).

Pusan Harbor is crowded with fishermen who return to shore to sell their catch. Pusan is South Korea's second largest city and a major port and industrial center in the southeast tip of the country.

The Southern Plain

This region lies south of the Central Mountain region and is made up of the more gently rolling hill lands and flood plain of the 325-mile-long (523-kilometer-long) Naktong River. At the coastline in the southeast, it runs from the Channel Cape by Yongil Bay and arcs around all the way to Kwangju in the west. The coastline is filled with small indentations that provide bays, sheltered coastlines for fishing, and the setting for countless small villages. The Korean Strait lies to the south of this plain and just beyond the Western Channel is Tsushima Island, the easternmost extension of Japan.

Nearly 25 percent of the South Korean population lives in the Southern Plain. This plain is rich in agriculture and serves as the "breadbasket" of the country because of its less harsh climate than in the north, and because of the relatively low relief, lying as it does south of the major mountain systems of the country. Pusan is the major industrial center in this region. But the Southern Plain exemplifies the full set of Korean landscapes. One can find coastal fishing villages, lowland agriculture focused on irrigated rice, soybeans, upland farming with other grains, sweet potatoes, and orchard fruits, and a generally fully developed land cover of human effort making the land productive at all elevations.

Cheju Island lies some 88 miles (142 kilometers) south of the coastline of the Southern Plain. It is a volcanic island and is home to the highest peak in South Korea, Mt. Halla. This mountain is 6,398 feet high (1,950 meters) and is an example of the scattered volcanism in this region of the Korean Peninsula. This area is part of the so-called Ring of Fire that arcs from western South and North America through East Asia all the way to the islands of Southeast Asia and New Zealand. It is characterized by volcanism and seismic instability (earthquakes). Mt. Halla and its stunning crater lake on Cheju Island play a ceremonial role in island culture as well as for the whole of South Korea. The island was called Quelpart during the colonial period, and the Japanese know this island as Saishu To.

The Southwestern Plain

This third major region makes up the rest of the generalized regions of South Korea. This plain stretches from the tip of South Korea and extends all the way to the Han River and its confluence with Kanghwa Bay to the west of Seoul. This is an even more significant farming and settlement region than the

Southern Plain and approximately one-half of the South Korean population lives in this region. Farming has been giving way slowly to the expanding urban base as the Southwestern Plain experiences the steady growth of Seoul and Inchon through continued economic development and industrial growth. The plain is thickly settled, with densities increasing progressively near the coastline and the northwest sector of South Korea.

This region is also important for the development of hydroelectric resources. Nearly 75 percent of South Korea's hydropower is generated on the Han River as it winds its way from its origin in the Taebaek Mountains and flows toward Kanghwa Bay on the western edge of this region. The Han River is only the fourth longest on the peninsula, but its abundance of water and relatively slow flow make it perfect for navigation, as well as for irrigation and hydroelectric power generation.

It is also in this region that South Korea experiences the majority of the mid- and late-summer typhoons that are so damaging to farming landscapes and settlements near the coastlines of the Southwestern and Southern Plains regions.

CLIMATE

Climate is a factor that gives character to all locales. In South Korea, the most dynamic climatic factor is the seasonal shift of winds caused by the fact that the peninsula is surrounded by the Sea of Japan, the Yellow Sea, the Korea Strait, and the massive East China Sea. Most of East Asia is powerfully influenced by the monsoon patterns that create summer periods of maximum precipitation and much drier winter seasons. The monsoon dynamic is basic to climate systems all through Asia and is the single most important element in the shaping of the climate of South Korea.

Urban areas continue to grow and expand in the Southwestern Plain. Increased economic development has caused towns to be established where there were once only farming communities.

The Monsoon Dynamic

The engine of all climate patterns is air mass movement. It is the differential temperatures of air masses that cause the steady lateral flow of massive bodies of air from one location to another. The catalyst for such steady movement is generally the differential heating of land vs. water.

The energy source for climate shift is always the sun, or

more exactly, insolation—the radiant energy received on the earth's surface from the sun. As the sun's rays pour down on earth, the temperature of the surface being warmed will heat generally at one rate if it hits land or rock or tree cover. However, the same amount of insolation (solar radiation) being brought to the sea, or a lake, or the ocean will have a distinct impact on the air temperature of that bit of the earth's surface.

Seas and ocean surround the Korean Peninsula. Although the Sea of Japan is much deeper than the Yellow Sea, both bodies of water absorb major amounts of insolation before they begin to warm in any way comparable to the land surface on the peninsula itself. When all of the landmass of China and Russia and the interior of the Asian continent is factored in, it is apparent that there is also an enormous land system absorbing the sun's energy being showered upon the Korean Peninsula.

At the same time, the surrounding bodies of water are receiving the same insolation but are dispersing it downward so that, as a result, the land gets much, much warmer in the high sun season—June to September—than do the adjacent water areas. Air masses move in response to differential temperatures with cooler, high-pressure air masses tending to move toward warmer, low-pressure air masses. The seasonal shift of winds moving from the sea surfaces toward the land surfaces in the wet season (April to September) and the reverse wind movement from the land toward the sea in the dry season (October to March) is the essence of the monsoon climate pattern. South Korea's climate is character-ized more by that influence than any other geographic factor.

With warm moist air being pulled from atop the surface of the sea by monsoon forces during the summer, it is the months of July, August, and September that have the heaviest rainfall of the year. The moist air masses flow from the sea toward the hot interior lands of the Asian continent during these high sun months. As such air masses are pulled up over the mountainous topography of the Korean Peninsula, the air cools, condenses, and areas that had only 2 to 6 inches (5 to 15 centimeters) of precipitation in March and April receive 10 to 14 inches (25 to 35 centimeters) in July and August.

In the low sun months of January and February, the monsoon forces are reversed. The sea surface is relatively warm (compared to the continental interior land masses of China and Inner Asia) and the flow of cold, high-pressure air masses rush toward the sea surfaces. As they flow across the Korean Peninsula and on toward Japan, moisture is picked up from the Sea of Japan—causing wet snows to fall on the west side of that island country. However, in both North and South Korea, the shifting air masses are intensely cold due to their source area in the depths of Asia. Since there is little moisture available for pick up in this reverse monsoonal flow, there is not as much snowfall as might be anticipated. The snowfall is most in the north and west of the peninsula. And, as is the case in most hilly and mountainous topography, there is more snowfall on higher elevations.

The average monthly temperature drops below freezing in South Korea except for in the coastal region of the Southern Plain. Seoul, in January, averages 23°F (-5°C) and in July the temperature is 78°F (25°C). At Pusan, the major port and industrial city in the southeast corner of the peninsula, January averages 35°F (2°C) and August, 78°F (25°C). In terms of precipitation, the average South Korean totals run from 40 to 55 inches (101 to 140 centimeters). Taegu—at the border of the Southern Plain and the Central Mountains in the southeast—has 38 inches (97 centimeters), and this is the driest part of the country. Pusan, lying on the coast to the southeast, has an average of 55 inches (140 centimeters) of precipitation annually. The difference comes from the fact that Pusan is the first landfall for the moist air masses moving in from the sea toward the warm land and the great pull of the China interior in the summer months. The range of frost-free days runs from 130 to 150 days in the northern part of the Korean Peninsula, but to as many as 225 in the south.

An additional factor that has major significance on the climate of South Korea is the occurrence of typhoons in the late summer. These destructive tropical storms move up from the Philippines in the summer and late summer and bring strong winds and enormous rainfall. Although they tend not to go very far inland, they pound coastal cities and villages and are a continual threat to summer harvests and buildings during the typhoon season.

PLANT AND ANIMAL LIFE

The Korean Peninsula has been settled, farmed, and moved across for thousands of years. Even though the landscape is only about one-fifth arable (land that can be farmed), the hallmarks of active settlement are clearly apparent in almost all prospects. The inventory of flora and fauna has been widely modified by the peninsula's corridor role in the ever-shifting interaction between the Asian continent and the Japanese archipelago (chain of islands). Whereas, for example, there used to be a fauna of bears, lynx, tigers, and leopards, these particular animals have become very rare. Deer and wild boar remain, but they have a steady struggle in staying free of the influence of expanding settlements.

South Korea is approximately 20 percent farmland with most of that located on the river plains and the lower elevation gradients of the Southern and Southwestern Plains that slope toward the Sea of Japan. The forest cover is a mix of coniferous trees and broadleaf subtropical forests. Because the peninsula of Korea extends across nine degrees of latitude (about 625 miles, or 1,006 kilometers) from Cheju Island in the south to the

Rivers provide irrigation for terraced rice paddies. Rice is a main crop and staple of the Korean diet. Growing rice is essential to the cultural and economic well-being of the Korean farmer and his family.

Yalu River in the north, there is considerable variation in the flora from north to south.

The landscape of Cheju Island in the Sea of Japan is the richest in variety. The most common trees include pine, maple, oak, larch, spruce, elm, willow, juniper, alder, birch, poplar, acacia, and bamboo. In addition, the country has an active orchard industry on the flatlands and mountain flanks, with the most important tree crops being apple, pear, peach, orange, tangerine, fig, and in the far south, the Chinese quince. These crops have been significant both to the domestic economy and for export trade to the lucrative Japanese market.

Fauna, as noted above, have diminished in number because of steadily expanding zones of human occupation of the Korean landscape. However, more than 350 species of birds have been recorded in South Korea. The heron, a spindly legged tall bird with a long narrow beak has been a focus in Korean poetry and paintings. It continues to be a landmark found on the southeast coast of the country. This bird is so important to the idealized images of South Korea that the government has established eight heronries for the breeding and protection of this elegant white bird.

The large mammals that remain a part of the Korean fauna in the south include the tiger, leopard, lynx—in small numbers—and the cat, wolf, badger, bear, marten, and roe deer. In everyday life, these animals are not easily found, but in a country that has a level of living that is improving and supporting ever more tourism, the maintenance of the environments that sustain all of these animals and birds becomes economically as well as environmentally more important every year.

THE SPIRIT OF PLACE IN SOUTH KOREA

When considering the location and setting for the Korean Peninsula and the particular historical geography of South Korea, it is quite impressive that the culture and history that will be investigated in the pages that follow is as distinctive as it is. The whole drama of Korea has been played out on a peninsula that has been an avenue for major cultural diffusion, attempted military invasions, and significant migration for thousands of years.

Lying as it does on the edge of China and Russia, and thrusting into the Sea of Japan, the Japanese archipelago, and the ocean currents that move both north and south from that region, Korea is a country that has had its natural landscapes shaped by the forces of the Ring of Fire. Its cultural landscapes are influenced by people and thought from many distant places.

The job now is to begin to piece together the different migrations and cultural transformations that have taken place through agriculture, human settlement, the growth of cities, and—more recently—dynamic economic development in South Korea.

The following chapter examines the flow of people through time to see what cultures, peoples, languages, and customs have been the most significant influences in creating the South Korea of the 21st century.

In 1259 the Mongol conqueror Genghis Khan, shown in this engraving, added Korea to his empire, which encompassed almost all of Eurasia.

South Korean Historical Geography

Humans are a species that is very fond of mobility. The typical teenager today travels from home to school, from school to recreation, from home to markets, from place to place to see friends, to go to shows, to go to events downtown. All of these little trips reflect the human fascination with mobility.

In thinking about that same motion over time, it is possible to quickly recall hearing about migrations over large distances. Previous generations came to the United States from Europe, Africa, Latin America, or Asia. All of those trips took enormous energy, dedication, courage, and probably money. It is one of the great truths: People are fond of mobility. And yet, even as the human potential for recurring movement is recalled, it must be acknowledged that people also become very fond of a place they call their own—a place they identify with as home, or their homeland.

To understand the Korean Peninsula, and South Korea in particular, it is important to begin by thinking, again, about the basic physical geography of the peninsula. The whole peninsula is a corridor of land that is about 86,000 square miles (222,000 square kilometers). That is about the size of the state of Minnesota or Michigan. This wedge of land is a peninsula off the eastern side of the largest continent in the world. It looks like a land bridge that goes out quite close (a little more than 100 miles, or 160 kilometers) to the Japanese islands. Those islands have long been seen as being part of a chain that facilitated the flow of ideas, foods, and peoples up and down the insular (isolated) world of East and Southeast Asia. Korea was the launch pad—or the receiving pad—to that world.

In addition, the Korean Peninsula lies between the two giants China and Russia; the dominant power of East Asia and the monumental Mongol power of north and inner Asia. It does not really lie between them, but the geography of that location has had it function somewhat as though it was territory that had to be dealt with if a raiding group or a warring group was moving across northern Asia toward China, toward Japan. For this reason, the history of Korea has been linked to the mobility of many other peoples and places.

When a geographer tries to determine what the patterns have been in the migration of a people, he or she looks for clues that might suggest origins. One of the most interesting features of the Korean Peninsula is that the Korean language is not related to Sino-Tibetan (which is the language of the Chinese peoples who are such a large proportion of the East Asian population). The Korean language is in a language family that includes Turkish, Hungarian, Japanese, and Finnish. The family is called Ural-Altaic, and it occurs in a broad band that stretches across the Eurasian continent. With Finnish and Hungarian as the westernmost examples, it then appears in Inner Asia and then comes to Manchuria and Korea and goes on to serve as the language base for Japanese.

The peoples of Korea are thought to be of a racial stock that was a blend of Caucasian and Asian stock characteristic of origins in the realm of current Kazakhstan in Central Asia. By approximately 4000–5000 B.C. these peoples had been through migration streams that had been working ever more eastward and reached the Korean Peninsula. The settlers who came in the Neolithic period—approximately 5,000–7,000 years ago—came already knowing of rice agriculture and bronze weapons and tools. They wore woven clothes (showing textile skills and advanced culture) and they already had developed village culture. One researcher, Kenneth Lee, describes them in this way: "It is known that the people of Korea were galloping horsemen, who moved swiftly, conquering any who stood in their way." The Chinese term for these people was the Tungu(s), or the Tungi.

Remember the image of the horse because the Ural-Altaic stock was the source of the Mongolian pastoralists (animal herders) who, in the middle of the 13th century A.D., created the largest empire that ever stretched across the breadth of Eurasia. The Mongols (Genghis and later Kublai Khan) controlled territory from the Korean Peninsula all the way to the edge of Poland in Eastern Europe. This stock is the same people who caused the Chinese to create their Great Wall. This limestone barrier nearly 1,500 miles long (2,414 kilometers) is a testimony to the fierceness with which these horse-riding warriors came into villages and raided them for food, supplies, and sometimes wives. The Koreans feel some pride in coming from such a people.

At the same time as peoples were coming from interior and Eastern Eurasia to the peninsula and settling several thousands of years ago, there was also a periodic crossing from Japan to the southern tip of the Korean Peninsula. There are large shell mounds showing fishing culture, and there is also evidence of rice cultivation. In one mound a Chinese coin from the second century B.C. was found as well. It is assumed that these settlements near the southern coast of the peninsula supported themselves by fishing, gathering in the hillside forests, some farming, and hunting.

In Chinese lore, there is also the story that a group of Chinese migrants left the northern Chinese Shang dynasty capital of An-yang. They crossed the Yalu River that separates the peninsula from China and proceeded to Pyongyang and founded a Chinese outlier community. According to East Asian scholar Albert Kolb,

> It was here in the northwest [of the Korean Peninsula] that China's five main crops, including rice and wheat, were introduced, and in time those crops and other products of Chinese culture began to spread. The native tribes gave up their foxtail millet wherever it was possible to introduce the new larger-grained cereals.

This continued the long-term exchange of life elements between the Chinese and the Koreans. General history has this cultural diffusion—the flow of cultural elements from one place to another—as going mostly from China to Korea and then on to Japan, but on balance it will be seen that there was diffusion going in a number of directions.

The Chinese made their first fully documented incursion into the Korean Peninsula at the very end of the second century B.C. In 108 B.C. they took over a major section of what is now North Korea, centering their control on the contemporary city of Pyongyang. This was followed by the formation of three states within the confines of the peninsula. The state of Koguryo was established in the northeast. Paekche was founded in the southwest. Silla was created in the southeast. This trio of states is the basis for the Three Kingdoms era in Korea, and it was well established by the 200s A.D.

These three kingdoms did not begin initially with a unified language or even cultural roots, although the peoples had come from the Altaic stock that had been moving across the plains of

The Pulguksa Buddhist Temple in Kyongju was constructed during the time of the unified Silla Kingdom in the 700s. It contains relics dating back to the eighth century.

Eurasia for ages. In this era of the three distinct regions—the east coast (Koguryo), the western lowlands south of Pyongyang (Paekche), and in the south (Silla)—it is said that there was no common language or unified land use. In the Koguryo region, there was still a strong forest tribe pattern. In Chinese records, it was noted that there was a more unified culture in the north—where the Chinese influence had been stronger.

As the Three Kingdoms period developed, the Koreans became a more coherent people and by 660 A.D. the Kingdom of Silla had grown strong enough to conquer both Paekche and Koguryo and unify the peninsula. Silla became stronger in its support of Confucianism, and this set the stage for even more

Chinese diffusion of cultural elements. This somewhat weakened the strength of a unified Korea.

By early in the 10th century, General Wang Kon unified the various sections of Korea and founded the Koryo government. This was in 932 A.D. and it was from this name that the country gained its current English name, Korea. It was under the power of this house that the world's first movable metal printing type was invented. This was achieved in 1234, or some two centuries before Johann Gutenberg is credited with first printing with movable metal type in 1436.

In the 1230s, the Mongols began a three-decade effort to conquer the Koryo government. In 1259 they finally succeeded and the Mongols took over the peninsula. This is the same time of the expansion of Genghis Khan, and later his grandson, Kublai Khan. Korea represented the easternmost margin of the Mongol empire. It ruled enormous areas of Eurasia until the end of the Yuan dynasty in China in 1368. The Mongols left Korea in the same year.

The Ming dynasty period in China (1368–1644) was a time of particular success for Korea, at least until near the end of the 16th century. The northern border of the Korean peninsula was pushed northward to the contemporary border of North Korea along the Yalu and Tumen Rivers.

This was the period of the Yi dynasty (1392–1910), and there is some important information particularly worth remembering about South Korea during this time:

In 1446, King Sejong developed the Korean alphabet. Historically, the Koreans—like the Japanese—had derived a good deal of their initial language from the written Chinese characters. In terms of spoken language, Korea had contesting tongues in all of the Three Kingdoms, but the Silla Kingdom had the strongest influence and from about the 7th century until the 10th century, Silla was the dominant language. All through this period, however, there was still a major influence from Chinese characters and style on the Korean tongue.

In about the middle of the 15th century there came to be a new interest in being able to get free of the Chinese dependency and develop a new Korean language. With extraordinary quickness, King Sejong of the Yi dynasty was the most important person in the development of the new—and distinctive— Korean language called Hangul. This is the only East Asian language that has an alphabet that is truly a cultural product of East Asia.

Although Hangul was not in use in 1234 when the first movable metal plate printing process was developed, the character nature (like Chinese and Japanese) of Hangul lent itself well to the press—particularly because the characters acted as an alphabet. That is, Hangul Korean has 19 distinct consonants, 10 vowels, and two glides, y and w. This is opposed to the thousands upon thousands of unique characters in the Chinese language, and nearly the same complexity in Japanese.

The invention and adoption of Hangul is another source of pride for both North and South Koreans as they attempt to become a major force in the global cultural as well as economic scene.

The rest of the Korean historical geography blends with the distinctive patterns of government and political history that will be described in Chapter 5.

Traditional South Korean families were often composed of up to three generations living in one house. Societal changes have led to fewer senior family members in the household and the need for facilities to care for older citizens.

4

South Korean People and Culture

I n thinking about population, it is important to realize that there is much more to that word than just the number of people. The elements that make up the image of a population include how people look, what they wear, what they eat, and how they entertain themselves. These traits are quite central to a geographer's study of a country, its people, and its culture.

This chapter outlines some of the factors that are vital to understanding population. It also characterizes South Korea in terms of those same elements.

Think of these descriptive traits of the current South Korean population.

Item	S. Korea Data	E. Asia* Data	World Rate
• Population:	49,000,000	1,503,000,000	–
• Births per 1,000 people annually	14	15	22
• Deaths per 1,000 people annually	5	7	9
• Rate of natural increase (RNI)	0.9	0.8	1.3
• Projected 2050 population total	51.1	–	–
• Infant mortality rate per 1,000	8	30	56
• Percent of population <15 years	22	22	30
• Percent of population >65 years	7	8	7
• Life expectancy at birth (avg.)	74	72	67
• Percent of population urban	79	42	46
• GNI PPP	$15,530	$5,750	$6,650

*East Asia is Japan, North and South Korea, China, Taiwan, Macao, and nearshore islands.

(Source: 2001 World Population Data Sheet. Population Reference Bureau)

What do these numbers mean? Every one of them reflects a major aspect of people and culture in the country of South Korea. Try to grasp what these statistics mean in relation to other people around the world. This will make it easier to understand many other points that are made throughout this book. One trait at a time will be explored. At the same time the South Korean reality in comparison with broader East Asia will be presented, and finally the data will be compared with the global picture.

Absolute Population

One of the first questions to ask about a country when just beginning to try to understand its importance is "How large is it?" The number of people living in a country tells something about its political significance, its economic importance and potential, its military power, and its possible concerns for feeding itself, for giving support to its population, and other things.

Absolute population is the key to at least beginning to under-stand these essential geographic elements. For example, what are the first traits thought of when China and India are mentioned?

In the context of East Asia, the 49 million people of South Korea may not seem like a very large population because there are more than 1.28 billion people in neighboring China, and Japan has a population of more than 130 million. If South Korea were compared, for example, with Minnesota, the results provide a keen sense of how many people there are in the South Korean world. The full Korean Peninsula (North as well as South Korea) has an area of some 85,400 square miles (221,186 square kilometers). That is almost the same area as the state of Minnesota. The Korean Peninsula has a combined population of more than 71 million, whereas Minnesota has just under 5 million population. Another way of seeing the impact of such population numbers is to know that South Korea has a national population density of 1,274 per square mile (453 per square kilometer). The figure for the entire United States is 78 per square mile (27 per square kilometer).

That is why population numbers are a good first step in understanding a place. From the very beginning of an analysis of South Korea, it is important to know that every government—from the most local city council to the national government—has the responsibility for finding shelter, employment, and support for many more people than in the United States or England. The ratio of population to political area (population density) is only a statistic, and it is sometimes confusing because major parts of a country can be desert and almost unpopulated. But as a first step, the absolute population and population density are vital to know.

Births Per 1,000 People Annually

Every government, like every family, has to deal with the people alive right now who are seeking support and information as well as jobs and accommodations. At the same time, however, there is always an additional pressure brought to bear on problem solving by the population growth rate, the fertility rate. This term—births per 1,000—is the indicator of the fertility rate of South Korea. This means that if this term is combined with the next one on the table (deaths per 1,000) the rate of natural increase (RNI) can be determined. It is this rate that is the most telling about the way in which a country has dealt with population.

Compare, for example, the fact that births for South Korea is 14; deaths is 5. For East Asia the two terms are 15 and 7. For the world, the average number of births is 22, deaths is 9. The RNI is 1.3 in South Korea, with a natural fertility rate of 0.8, which is approximately one-half the world average. Population growth is not simply the issue of providing for the current population. For countries experiencing rapid population growth, it is having to produce such services at an ever faster rate, because their population is growing so quickly. South Korea has managed to slow its population growth rate with considerable efficiency.

Projected 2050 Population

This relatively low growth from 49 million to just over 51 million in the next half century brings considerable pride to the South Korean government. This figure is important to government planners in South Korea. When planning for growth and economic development, if the population grows too quickly, most of the projects undertaken in new highways, jobs, apartment buildings, and schools seem just to vanish. A stable population like the one suggested in this table is good news for the government. It helps spotlight the development that the government has funded and constructed.

Infant Mortality Rate

Think of the traits that are represented by an index of infant mortality. Everything from a country's health system, the average health of the people themselves, the educational levels of expectant mothers, the provision of food for mothers and for new children—all of these factors play a major role in the

Korean children are shown here dancing in traditional dress. The government has to plan for the education, housing, and employment of South Korea's increasingly urban future generations.

rate of infant mortality. The East Asian average is 30 per 1,000, a figure that is nearly four times as high as the South Korean rate. The world average is 56, or seven times higher than South Korea. Such a low infant mortality rate is the hallmark of a strong and healthy population.

Population Under the Age of 15

The next two numbers are simple numbers, but each has a strong implication for government policy and future aspects of economic development. South Korea has just over one-fifth of its population under the age of 15. Twenty-two percent of its population is just coming of age, ready to get education and then a career. This population of children looking for these two things represents a foundation of opportunity and responsibility for South Korea. These youth are the future workers and leaders of the country. But they also are a population that has to be accommodated. The East Asian average is identical with South Korea, and the world average is one-third again as high. This is more evidence of the fact that South Korea has managed its population with some success.

Population Over the Age of 65

The other number is the opposite end of the age scale. South Korea has only 7 percent of its population over 65 years of age. This is called the dependency population, or the people who will have probably stopped working and who will be needing places that can care for them. In the traditional South Korean family, these senior people—the parents, the grandparents, and the senior uncles and aunts—used to be housed in the extended families that were customary in Korean culture (as in Chinese and Japanese cultures as well). But, new demographic patterns have led to the collapse of the family that used to have two or even three generations living in the same house. Young Korean families, particularly in cities, are now made up of the husband and wife and their own children. Fewer and fewer families house parents and grandparents. This means that there has developed a real social need for places and personnel that can take care of those who are over 65.

Life Expectancy at Birth

South Korea's average life expectancy of 74 (females 78 and males 71) is above both the East Asian and the world average. This, like the index for infant mortality, indicates that public health and government services are well developed. Considering that 50 years ago South Korea was deeply involved in a costly and disruptive war, the progress that such figures and traits demonstrate is truly remarkable.

The final two statistics are more closely related than they appear at first glance. The linkage between these final two characteristics is one that has a continual influence on national efforts at economic development.

Percent of Population Living in Cities

This index deals with the percent of South Korean population that lives in cities. More than 75 percent of the country's people are urban residents. This means that they are likely to have higher levels of education, to be more keenly aware of potential consumer benefits of living in the city, and have smaller families. The impact of this means that, in most cases and in most places, Korean youth give more attention to the benefits of having fewer or no children than they ever have before in the country's history.

The GNP PPP

Perhaps the most telling statistic in this table is the last one. The Republic of South Korea has an annual gross national product purchasing power parity (GNP PPP) of $15,530. The world average is $6,650. South Korea has been able to bring its level of per capita purchasing power up to two and a half times the world average—and this is less than 50 years after a truly devastating war with North Korea and Mainland China. This economic success is a source of enormous pride to the leaders and people of South Korea. They see this as a reflection of forceful leadership and dedication by people of all levels ever since the completion of World War II, and more significantly, since the 1953 end of the Korean Conflict.

DEMOGRAPHIC SHIFTS

In the evolving changes in patterns of people and culture, few things have been as important in South Korea as the demographic shifts that have taken place in the past half-century. Consider, for example, these statistics:

Changes in Non-Urban to Urban Setting in South Korea

Year	Percent Urban	Percent Non-Urban
1925	5	95
1940	25	75
1960	28	72
1980	53	47
1990	74	26
2000	82	18

The distribution pattern that begins the chart, with the vast majority of South Koreans living in the countryside and making their living in agricultural labor, is typical of most of East Asia and much of the less developed world at the time. Even by 1940, the country had changed to only a 25:75 ratio with still more than two-thirds of the population engaged in rural labor and rural living.

In 1950, South Korea adopted a military conscription system that began the change that is now fully dominant all across the country. Korean males, once they reach the age of 20, are required to spend two years in military service. This enactment had a great deal to do with the Korean Police Action (as the 1950–1953 Korean War is called), but the changes that this conscription initiated have continued until today.

Two major changes came from this demographic shift. First of all, when all young men know that they have a date with two years of army service as soon as they are 20 years old, they are inclined to put off the idea of early marriage. Two things happen with this decision. One of them is obvious; the other is a little more surprising.

The obvious one is that the average age of married couples goes up all across the country. Men are older and generally into the early or mid-20s before marriage. Women generally tend to be younger than the men that they marry, but they, too, are at an average age of high teens to low 20s when they are married. The combination of these two factors and the subsequent older marriage age gives the couple a somewhat shorter span of childbearing years—but that is insignificant compared to another more surprising result of this age shift.

The young Korean men who came in from the rural world for these years of military service had generally very limited urban experience. To them the city world associated with their military posts—or at least their leaves and R and R (rest and recreation)—was not only different from their youth, it was extraordinarily different.

A young man who had been raised, for example, on Cheju Island off the southwest coast and was then posted to some base in Kyonggi Province north of Seoul suddenly found himself exposed to a great range of urban attractions (and fears) that were not part of his island life. This exposure leads to fast learning and, generally, to a growing fascination with the breadth of opportunities that are associated with the city setting. This fascination—although it is always mixed and never simply an infatuation with urban delights—is the surprising factor for it is this new preoccupation with becoming a success in the city that has a real impact on the current patterns of population growth in South Korea.

THE CHANGING MIND-SET

It is the new interest in the demands and returns of success in urban life that have had the greatest impact on the changing fertility rates in the Korean population. As noted above, marriage takes place somewhat later because of these years in the military, but it is not only time that has passed, there are traditions that are left behind in this particular shift in mind-set. The young man who may have been a farmer's third son on Cheju Island now finds himself more free of the rural base because he spent these years away from home.

South Korean men must serve two years in the military, beginning at age 20. Here mounted military cadets are shown during a graduation ceremony in Seoul.

At the same time, he has seen things in those years, in those experiences, and in his conversations with so many other young men (and women in the cities) that he gives thought to a future that may not be built around getting married immediately, having children quickly, or trying to continue family traditions on a small farm. Rather, there come images of a salaried job in the city, education, or possible business ventures. All of these new possibilities are hampered by young children and the expenses of having and supporting a family in the city.

Suddenly a whole traditional pattern is called into question, and traditions begin to weaken. It is this change that has been most responsible for reducing fertility rates in South Korea to their current low levels as shown in the table on page 42. And the reduction of a country's average fertility rate has an impact on economic development, which is a topic that will be examined after a discussion of government.

The entire question of population is central to all other aspects of development and political—as well as economic—success in the contest of nations that will characterize the 21st century in East Asia and beyond. The South Koreans have been quite successful in their reduction of natural fertility, their accommodation of rural to urban migration, and their efforts to provide education and jobs for their young adults. The challenge of finding ways to support the population that is over 65 is, and will be increasingly, a test of the growing country's creativity and social efficiency.

PEOPLE AND CULTURE

The people of South Korea (like the people of the entire Korean Peninsula) have an extraordinarily homogeneous past. As noted earlier, South Korea is 99.9 percent Korean stock, and the very tiny additional group is mostly Chinese. While there are also some Japanese, the cultural tradition in East Asia has long been—with the exception of the Chinese of the southeast coastal areas—to maintain roots in the mother country. If a migration is undertaken, it is almost always defined as "sojourning," or going abroad to get education or make money, but the plan is then to return and reestablish roots in the country of one's birth.

It is thought that the initial migrations into the Korean Peninsula came from the north, and northwest. Lore—and anthropology—has stories of origins in the Altaic mountains of Central Asia. This tradition is supported by the fact that the Korean language shows connections with Altaic stock and not Sino-Japanese languages.

There is also a lesser, but consequential, migration path that has moved from the Shandong Peninsula of China, across the Yellow Sea, and into the western shores of the Korean Peninsula. This route was well known two or three thousand years ago, but it may also have introduced migrating peoples in the Korean Peninsula during the Neolithic period.

As was noted in previous chapters, the Japanese have also been important in their encroachments on Korea. They were of dominant importance from 1910 until the end of World War II. They were also closely involved with Korean efforts to exclude Western influences in the 17th- to mid-19th centuries. The Japanese were, with the French and Americans, most significant in opening Korea to new trade and cultural exchange after the 1870s.

The cultural characteristics of South Korea have their origins in agricultural society. Close-knit families, with two or even three generations living together in the same farm household were the tradition for centuries. People with the same, common surnames such as Park, Kim, or Lee did not ordinarily marry each other but there was still not a great deal of inter-village migration. Land ownership, for example, was a stabilizing factor and whole family histories were tied to such traditional resources as land, position in the farming community, and a broad-scale belief in Confucian customs of ancestor worship and nearly religious support of one's parents and elders.

Although these same patterns have some continuity in the rural countryside of South Korea, the whole demographic shift from a rural setting to an urban setting (the country is now more than 80 percent urban) has prompted a profound cultural shift. What had been a culture derived from the proximate Chinese, and to a lesser degree, Japanese, has now become more closely linked to Western society and Western industrial traits. There has been a more rapid evolution of Korean culture in the past 50 years than at anytime in the prior five centuries.

What does it mean to say that culture has been changed by the demographic shift from the countryside to the city? It means, for example, that the traditional farm custom of having grandparents and parents live with their children who are raising their own families cannot be carried into the city. Urban space is at a premium and both expensive and difficult to secure.

Cultural patterns that promoted large numbers of children in the rural world where they could play an active role in farm life no longer are common. Children cost more money because of space costs and material needs in the city—and they do not have the same set of productive chores they can accomplish as in the rural sector.

Women, who would only seldom have considered a career or working life from the farm base of the past, now have more education and more job opportunities. A change like this is a powerful force rippling through the cultural fabric of South Korea and it touches virtually all segments of contemporary society.

In language and religion, these same forces of change occur as well. The Korean language is a source of pride to both the South and North Koreans. When it was devised in the middle of the 15th century it served as a significant break from the endless and sometimes stifling presence of overwhelming Chinese influence on the Korean Peninsula.

Modern cities and shopping districts are becoming more common. The shift toward urban areas and away from rural villages has caused cultural changes for the society.

Prior to the development of Hangul, the Koreans had built their written language around Chinese characters (much as the early Japanese had also done). But, with the invention of the 24 Hangul characters in the 1400s, the Koreans gained a new independence.

In terms of religion, South Korea today has no official religion and, in fact, some 50 percent of the population claims not to have a religious preference. Of the other half, approximately half are Buddhist, half are Christian of whom about 6 percent are Catholic. This religious pattern has been carried to the United States as Korean immigrants move to American cities. Signs written in Korean have appeared in churchyards as these new populations establish a social base to help support the recently arrived immigrants from South Korea.

Confucian influences are still felt to some degree. Koreans who may belong to Protestant or Catholic churches may also, at home, still give some attention to Confucian customs. Even though the Chinese generally claim that Confucianism is not a religion, this belief system that has an influence on social custom is often mentioned in religious discussions. In South Korea it is still a presence, although very minor in scale in any formal terms.

So, with a basic understanding of the interplay of people, language, religion, and history, what have the South Koreans done to organize their country in political terms? What patterns have they established to put these creative and expressive traits in order? Such questions will be considered in the following chapter on the South Korean government.

President Kim Dae Jung (center) and first lady Lee Hee Ho (left) greeted South Korea's new prime minister, Chang Sang (right) in Seoul in July 2002. President Kim won the 2000 Nobel Peace Prize for improving human rights in his country.

South Korean Government

I n looking at the world through the eyes of a geographer it is common to begin any observation and analysis with themes of location, physical setting, and resource patterns. In the case of South (and North) Korea, it is important to remember that the Korean Peninsula has, for all historical time, existed as an avenue of military and cultural movement from east to west and from west to east. Virtually all Korean patterns of government and political history have been powerfully shaped by the location of the Korean Peninsula between the world of Japan and the Pacific, and of China, Russia, and Inner Asia on the north and west.

What does this mean? The Chinese influences in early kingdoms and in the important years of the kingdoms of Koguryo, Silla, and Paekche (75 B.C. to 932 A.D.) were the strongest influence in the development of the Korean government. With the success in 932 A.D. of a new government that called itself Koryo, the peninsula gave education new importance and in 1234 the world's first movable metal printing type was invented in Korea. This innovation was created in order to communicate more efficiently with the people of the Koryo government.

In 1392 came the Yi dynasty and with this came a new importance for Buddhism. For the following centuries there was continued tension between the Chinese, the Japanese, and the Manchus of Northern China. During these troubled times, the Korean Peninsula served as a theater for military campaigns, religious competition, and political control. These forces have been part of the dynamics of the Korean setting all through the peninsula's history.

DATES OF MAJOR POLITICAL SIGNIFICANCE

Although geography is keenly concerned with place, it is also attentive to dates and the sequences of change in a place's history. The following dates are benchmarks for building an understanding of those influences that have led to the present South Korean government.

108 B.C.

This is the year when the Chinese first established a formal state in Korea. This state amounted to the northern half of the peninsula. It was divided into three districts that ultimately became the Three Kingdoms. There were continual battles between the Chinese and the various Korean territories that fought to be free of Chinese control. This battling went on for centuries, and the major forces were the Korean kingdoms of Koguryo in the north, Paekche in the southwest, and Silla in the southeast. There was also a much smaller region called Kaya that existed around the present-day Pusan in the southern end of the peninsula.

313 A.D.

In this year, the various Korean forces drove the Chinese out of the peninsula and Buddhism was introduced in 372 A.D. This era is often known as part of the Three Kingdoms period (57 B.C.–668 A.D.). As a part of the government of this period, a legal code modeled after the Chinese was established. The old capital was moved from far north Korea to the site of today's North Korean capital, Pyongyang. In addition, the first Korean university was founded and a pattern of Chinese agricultural taxes and mass group labor was adopted. It is clear from all of this borrowing that even through this Three Kingdom period (Koguryo in the north; Paekche in the southwest; and Silla in southeast), the source of many things relating to government in Korea was Chinese.

918

The Koryo dynasty was founded in 918. This was the most unified Korean government that the peninsula had seen in centuries. The Koreans spent considerable effort and money in the building and moving to a new capital city called Kaesong (also known as Hansong) just north and west of present-day Seoul in South Korea. This new city was modeled after the traditional Chinese capital city of Chang-an (present day X'ian in northern China). It had the great urban checkerboard grid pattern that was so typical of Chinese governmental cities. To further establish the power of the Chinese models for government, the Chinese examination system for the selection of governmental officials was instituted in 958.

1259

In this year the Mongol armies that had conquered China and established themselves as the Yuan (Mongol) dynasty also extended their control over Korea. From this base one of the ongoing Mongol efforts was to cross the Sea of Japan that lies around and to the east of Korea and invade Japan. Three efforts in the years 1261, 1274, and 1281 failed, but Mongol control was maintained over Korea.

1392

Nearly four centuries of Koryo dynasty (but a century of that was fundamentally Mongol control) supremacy ended with the ascension of Yi Song-gye and the beginning of the Yi dynasty. It had basic control of the peninsula until 1910. Then the Japanese became the new East Asia superpower and took over basic control of Korea. During the Yi dynasty, Korea established "tribute status" with China's Ming dynasty. This meant that Korea accepted the reality that China was the dominant political—and cultural and military—power of the region. It also meant that Korea would provide financial support to China but would, in return, be favored by military and cultural support from China.

One of the most dramatic things done by the new Koryo government (besides providing the word for the current name for the peninsula, Korea) was the establishment of a totally new land tenure system. In General Yi Song-gye's drive at the beginning of his new dynasty, he confiscated and burned all of the land registers in 1390. This, in essence, turned all of the Korean farmland into a resource controlled by the new dynasty. Yi gave—in classic traditional fashion—the best lands and the lands closest to the seat of power to his most dedicated and trustworthy subordinates. The produce of these lands was used to support the Yi dynasty's governmental bureaucracy.

In the redistribution of the lands farther away from the capital city, lands were given to the second tier of supporters, and these lands were used to support the military. This process meant that the military had primary interest in the continued productivity of the outer ring of farmlands while the government (with its own additional military garrisons)

This farmhouse was built during the Yi dynasty. General Yi Song-gye destroyed records of land ownership and redistributed the best farmland to his closest allies.

kept strong control of the inner circle of productive Korean farmlands. In both cases, this burning of the traditional land ownership records reduced, or eliminated, the potential political power of the landowners who might have been least inclined to see a new government take control at the outset of the Yi dynasty.

This process was particularly important in Korea. In the centuries prior to the Yi dynasty, Korean landowners were, in essence, the very power of the state. This land redistribution opened the door for major changes in political authority in the peninsula.

1640

Over the course of the first three centuries of the Yi dynasty, the Japanese had been continually active in efforts to control Korea. In the 1590s, several invasions were undertaken and, at the outset, were successful. However, through strong and continuing resistance the Koreans were able to drive the Japanese back to their island empire to the east.

In the 1630s, the Manchus of northern China attacked Korea and were able to occupy seats of government because of their location and the force of their military troops. This is the same military power that would later seize political power from the Chinese Ming dynasty in 1644. In Korea, the traditional role of king was maintained, even if power really rested in the Chinese-Manchu government. The Manchus turned the great majority of their concern to China proper in an effort to secure this much larger prize in the East Asian realm in the middle of the 17th century.

The year 1640 is most important for Koreans. In that year the Yi government closed the Korean Peninsula to all foreign trade except a tightly controlled interaction with the Ch'ing dynasty of China. This began two centuries of Korean isolation from virtually all foreign influences. The self-imposed seclusion earned the country the name "The Hermit Kingdom." This effort was meant to keep foreign missionaries, merchants, and personnel beyond reach of the Korean peoples and landscape—and, most importantly, to isolate Korean culture.

During this period a wooden palisade was constructed along the Yalu and Tumen Rivers at the northern boundary of Korea. No foreign trade was allowed and efforts to achieve such trade through leaving the country were punishable by death. Only one ship a year was allowed into Korea, and that was the ship from Peking, China. Foreign sailors who made it to Korean land were interned (confined) or worse, and Korean sailors who violated this law of isolation were put to death.

1876

In the 236 years that Korea closed it borders and denied its fishermen and sailors access to the broader outside world, the global scene changed profoundly. The Age of Discovery, with its associated colonization of countries on all continents (except Antarctica) by European naval and trading powers, had accelerated the diffusion of Western military techniques, industrial patterns, religious belief systems, and popular culture. Japan had also pulled its borders in and had, like Korea, experienced more than two centuries of self-imposed closure.

In 1853–1854, the United States effectively opened the Japanese island nation by sending Commodore Matthew Perry at the head of a squad of four ships (two of which were very powerful steam frigates) into Yokohama (then Yedo) harbor requesting that the Japanese government allow the United States to buy coal in Japan. In addition, the United States also wanted assurance that shipwrecked American sailors on Japanese shores would be well treated. Finally, it demanded that Japan open ports other than Nagasaki to foreign trade.

The Japanese, with great reluctance, agreed to these terms in early 1854 and soon thereafter began to break down the closure of Korea. The French had made an ineffective effort to force Korea open in 1866, and America tried the same in 1871, with the same result. Finally in February 1876, the Japanese forced a treaty upon the Koreans, and Korea opened its coast to a new era of foreign trade and interaction.

As a result of the first Sino-Japanese War in 1894–1895 and the Russo-Japanese War of 1904–1905, the political landscape in East Asia was changing profoundly. From Japan's 1854 opening and its 1878 Meiji restoration (a bold effort at major modernization led by the Japanese government), it had engineered a monumental political power swing away from China and Russia. And, as has been so often the case, Korea's political future and reality were changed in direct relationship to those two Japanese military victories.

By 1910, Japan had ended the Yi dynasty that had been the basic governmental force in Korea for more than five centuries. It had also taken the Korean Peninsula under its military, economic, and cultural wing after the resignation of a pro-Russian Korean emperor. From the Japanese came an edict that the country was now to be ruled by a governor general as part of the (expanding) Japanese empire.

1945

At the conclusion of the World War II, changes in East Asia came about quickly and had enormous impact on the next half century. Russia came very late to the Pacific theater of World War II in 1945, but when the Japanese surrendered after an atom bomb was dropped on Nagasaki on August 9, the Russians gained a firm foothold in the Korea that lay north of the 38th parallel on the peninsula. U.S. troops secured the lands of South Korea as the Japanese were sent home. For two years the United States and Russia attempted unsuccessfully to overcome the territorial division on the peninsula. In 1947 the United States submitted this political issue to the newly formed United Nations (UN) in an effort to show what the new world organization could accomplish. However, 55 years have passed and the peninsula is still divided.

By 1949 the Russian and American troops had withdrawn from their sectors in both Koreas, but in June 1950, the North

After the North Korean Army invaded the south in June 1950, soldiers such as these from South Korea mobilized to fight the Communist threat.

Korean army invaded South Korea and the three-year Korean Conflict began.

1950

It is impossible to know exactly what caused the North Koreans to spill across the 38th parallel and invade South Korea. The Russian troops had left the north, the Americans had left the south. The North Korean regime under Kim Il Sung had been put in place by the Soviets in their efforts to diminish the new American presence in East Asia. Kim had rejected out of hand all efforts to reunify North and South Korea in the last years of the 1940s. In June 1950, Kim's forces came across the 38th parallel and quickly took a commanding position over the smaller and less well trained and equipped army of South Korea.

Concerned about what had happened in the early stages of the European theater in World War II, U.S. President Harry Truman decided that action more than words had to characterize American response to this very real threat of Soviet expansion in war-torn East Asia. Ironically, the Soviet Union was at that time boycotting the UN Security Council because of the UN failure to recognize the Communist People's Republic of China as the official holder of the Chinese seat in the UN. Accordingly, President Truman had the United States present the position that North Korea was the aggressor in their crossing of the dividing line and—with the United States promising to provide troops—the UN undertook a "police action" to bring an end to the Korean Conflict.

And—in one of the most costly absences for the Soviet Union in their UN history—because the Soviet representative was not present at this vote to declare North Korea the aggressor, the motion passed. Since a single negative vote in the UN Security Council will stop any action, the Korean War was initiated only because of this rare empty Soviet seat around the meeting table.

There was bitter fighting, and a very clever and unexpected military maneuver by General Douglas MacArthur (who had spent the prior five years heading the American occupation of Japan as part of the conclusion of World War II) turned the tide, and the army of the UN and South Korea pushed the North Korean invading troops north of the 38th parallel. More importantly, the MacArthur success in a daring amphibious landing at Inchon—just southwest of Seoul—led to a changing flow of the Korean armies. As a result, China got worried and in November 1950, hundreds of thousands of Chinese volunteers came into the Korean Conflict.

To the Chinese, the UN forces looked as though they were on a clear track that would lead to the invasion of their northeast (Manchuria) industrial zone. This region was the heartland of China's heavy industry factories and resources. Although the United States proclaimed that it was not interested in crossing into China, the Chinese responded with powerful military campaigns to push the UN forces back to a point just north of the 38th parallel again.

General MacArthur wanted to take the battle right into China. He believed that China, especially allied with Russian forces and resources, was going to turn the hard fought victory in the Pacific theater of war into a chaos of Communism. He saw that the force represented by his troops and the UN-mandated forces was powerful and already in a position to defeat or at least weaken Communist China. A smashing hit to the industrial heartland just beyond the border of North Korea (the Yalu River) could be accomplished and define the American presence in East Asia in the most forceful possible way.

President Truman felt that America was tired to its core after four years of a heavy and costly war that it had fought— and won. He felt that the UN effort in Korea was intended to be limited to a reestablishment of the divide between North and South Korea that had been created at the end of WWII. He refused to give MacArthur permission to push his troops further north. MacArthur rejected this restraint, so Truman fired him. The costs of this police action were not only the 54,000 American troop deaths, the 2 million Korean war dead, the 100,000 Americans wounded—but also the first major stand-off between the America Executive Office and the American military in decades.

In 1953 an armistice was finally signed that involved the 15 UN member nations that had sent troops to the Korean

U.S. Army General Mark W. Clark (center) signed the armistice agreement in 1953 that ended the Korean War. He was surrounded by members of the United Nations negotiating team.

Peninsula, and North Korea and the Soviets. The great majority of the forces had been American, yet it was only in 2001 that a major tribute was created in Washington, DC, for the war dead. The struggle for reunification of North and South Korea continues up to the present. This situation serves as a reminder that so-called short-term boundary changes that are initiated because of the unexpected outcomes of military actions and associated political contests may cost many lives and may exist for decades.

This series of dates and associated governmental characteristics provide a sense of the variety of influences that have been instrumental in the development of government and politics that led the Korean Peninsula into the middle of the 20th century. The two nations in that divided peninsula have each had a profoundly different second half of the last century, and the South Korean pattern will be the focus of the remainder of this segment on government in Korea.

CHINESE INFLUENCES ON KOREAN HISTORY

China was the most powerful influence on Korean history from 108 B.C. to the beginning of the 20th century. There has been no country or civilization that has come close to having the same impact as has Korea's major neighbor to the northwest. To bring into focus such influences as the discussion turns to the more recent, and less China-oriented development in South Korea since 1950, consider this quote from the comprehensive study of East Asia by Reishauer and Fairbank.

> A still more important reason for the difference between Korea and China may have been that Confucian philosophy and the Chinese political system had originated with the Chinese but had only been borrowed by the Koreans. The Chinese, as originators of the whole system, may have retained more capacity for adjustment and innovation. ... The Koreans, as the borrowers of a ready made system ... adopted Confucian ritual forms with a literalness that far surpassed the Chinese. This literal and sometimes blind acceptance of Chinese ideas naturally proved stultifying to intellectual development. It took even greater courage to be an innovator ... in Korea than in China itself. ... Another factor may have been the orientation of all Confucian thought and, with it, all Korean education toward China and its classical language, rather than toward Korea and the native language. As a result, most Korean minds tended to be drawn away from immediate realities [448–449].

This reminder that the overarching influence of China was already a reality must be remembered when considering the last half-century of South Korea's government and its political systems.

THE YEARS AFTER 1953

In 1948, Syngman Rhee had been elected president of South Korea. There had been a steady effort to reunify the peninsula—promoted both by the United States and the Soviet Union—but when that was clearly not going to happen, each country went in its own direction. One of the assessments of the development of South Korean politics has been to represent the recent decades as a period of the Six Republics. Consider these different periods of development.

The First Republic (1948–1960)

From 1948 until 1960, South Korea was headed by Syngman Rhee, first elected in 1948 and, through a variety of political moves (including constitutional amendments and a long history of political dependence upon the central government), Rhee was able to stay in power until April 1960. He and his government had been reelected again that year, but uprisings among students and the general population became so strong that he resigned that month. New public elections were held in July 1960 and this began the next government.

The Second Republic (1960–1961)

The government was led by President Chang Myon, but his regime was weakened by the increasingly strong rivalry of political groups, and Chang's government never really was able to establish a firm base for this republic. In 1961 he was overthrown by a military coup headed by General Park Chung Hee. In an unusual move, Park called for democratic elections in 1963, and his government won the election with General Park as president.

The Third and Fourth Republics (1962–1980)

Park and his government gave much attention to economic development (see the next section), and he was able to win reelection in 1967 and again in 1971. With further amendments to the South Korean constitution, Park was able to run for president again (and again) and was reelected in 1978. Between his last victory and his assassination in 1979, the United States began a slow pull out of the 38,000 troops that it still had stationed in South Korea. Following the death of Park came the new government of Choi Kyu-hah. In 1981, Ronald Reagan was took the office of president of the United States, and he stopped the troop withdrawal from South Korea.

The Fifth Republic (1980–1988)

Under the new government of Choi Kyu-hah, the major power source for the South Korean government was Chun Doo Hwan. Because the government of Park had promised a constitutional revision that would have allowed the direct election of the president—but the subsequent government of Chun had not permitted this amendment—there began a period of civil unrest. In May 1980, Chun and the military forces declared martial law. Although Choi remained the titular president, real authority was in the offices of Chun Doo Hwan, and new restrictions on freedom of assembly and speech were enforced.

After a number of bloody confrontations during this period of martial law, President Choi resigned and Chun Doo Hwan was elected by the electoral college as the new president in 1980. In 1981 martial law was repealed. In 1987, President Chun raised the promise yet again of a constitutional amendment that would allow the direct election of the next president. In 1988, Roh Tae Woo—also an ex-general and a close associate of Chun Doo Hwan—was elected as president under the new constitution.

The Sixth Republic (1988–1993)

Not only was the election of Roh Tae Woo the most direct ever known in South Korea, there were also significant new civil liberties established, and these allowed unprecedented political freedom. Part of the impact of these new political freedoms was an increased number of strikes and worker protests regarding wages, working conditions, and benefits. This all led to a slowdown in the rapidly growing South Korean economy. These changes led to a partial economic stagnation of the development forces during the five years (1988–1993) of Roh's presidency. However, the civil changes set in motion during his presidency led to a major increase in local political authority and greater freedom of the press, and set the stage for the first nonmilitary government South Korea had known since 1960. With the inauguration of Kim Young Sam in February 1993, civilian government was reopened and with it, the current era of a more democratic government in South Korea.

With the initiation of the presidency of Kim Young Sam, the government moved toward an elimination of fraud in elections and real reform of campaigns, finances, and governmental bureaucracy. One of the most impressive aspects of this change came in 1995 when, for the first time since 1961, local and provincial governmental officials were elected by direct vote of the local citizens. This meant that some 15,700 officials—from mayors to provincial governors to local officials—were elected. Included in this new wave were 15 provincial governors and mayors of major cities.

In 1998 Kim Dae Jung was inaugurated, and he was the first president to come from some other political party than the New Korea Party (which had been called the Democratic Liberal Party until 1995). Although Kim's margin was slim, the fact that he was elected at all seems to indicate that political authority was, in fact, being more broadly distributed through the ranks of the Korean population.

President Kim Dae Jung began to define his presidency by what is sometimes called his "sunshine policy." This was a series of political overtures his government made to North Korea in an effort to open the door to increased travel, trade, and political interaction between North and South Korea. It was also hoped that the political climate would change enough to be able to craft a final treaty to the 1950–1953 Korean War. In the year 2000, President Kim received the Nobel Peace Prize for these efforts and others relating to improving human rights in South Korea.

At the beginning of the 21st century there was still no resolution to the open declarations of war that had come out of the 1950 attack of North Korean forces on South Korean territory south of the 38th parallel.

The whole dynamic of government and politics in South Korea is a reflection of the major international issues relating to the proximity of China, Japan, and Russia and other countries. At the same time, local conditions and the politics of local, provincial, and national governments are continually influential on the nature of South Korean governmental policy. There are at least two scales to be considered in the understanding of these major issues that shape the pattern and characteristics of the South Korean landscape and scene. Just as this has been true in government, it is even more evident in the consideration of economic issues and economic geography.

Small businesses in the cities sell a variety of household items, food, and clothing. These independent business owners make up an increasingly important segment of the urban population.

CHAPTER

6

The Economy
of South Korea

I n thinking about the economic activities of any country, remember that there are many different settings to understand. Think about an American household. While parents will have the economic activity they undertake to support the household, children in a family also make their own contributions. For example, one parent may be a lawyer, while the other parent is a teacher. That does not mean that their children do not try to earn money with babysitting or lawn work or part-time work in a local business.

Beyond the family unit, the state has a number of very significant economic activities—just as is true of cities or rural areas. Carried one step further, it becomes apparent that there are dominant national exports and products and skills that characterize the picture of a country. This shift from scale to scale, from level to level, is what a lot of education is about. There is always an effort to build on what is known at the local level and then learn how to add to that picture and develop an understanding of the bigger picture.

In the case of South Korea, this scale change is keenly important.

THE ECONOMIC GEOGRAPHY OF SOUTH KOREA

One researcher, in assessing what it is that has made the South Korean economy do so very well in the last several decades, came up with this list of factors—most of which relate to the four landscapes under consideration in this chapter. Ironically, this list was created in response to questions from the Chinese who wanted to have their giant nation find a way to undergo development in a pattern parallel to the 1960s and 1970s successes in South Korea.

These Seven Guidelines for Economic Development were presented in *The US–Korea Economic Partnership* by Kim and Oh as follows:

1. Adopt a very powerful work ethic;
2. Achieve a high degree of excellence in education, at all levels—primary, secondary and advanced;
3. Provide good working opportunities for well-trained young people, encouraging them not to join the brain-drain group [that is, the youth who go abroad for their college and graduate education but do not return to South Korea];
4. Live sparingly for many years, saving a high fraction of income;
5. Be moderate and fair in wage demands, especially in the early stages of expansion;
6. Be good hosts to foreign enterprises who can supply advanced technology; and
7. Seek out world markets.

The exploration of four local scenes will reveal how well

this list does in providing an explanation for the success of the South Korean economy.

Local Economic Geography

There are four worlds to think about when trying to imagine and understand the South Korean economic landscape.

The Korean farmer

One of the landscape traits that bonds the people of East Asia and Southeast Asia—the Chinese, Japanese, Korean, Vietnamese, and many others—is the peasant farming scene. It is generally made up of simple households with a minimum of wasted space around the wooden home and its unpainted out-buildings. There will almost always be a "kitchen garden" that is the resource base used by the peasant household for vegetables and sometimes flowers for decorating and pleasure.

The fields closest to the home structure are farmed with great care. They are usually given over to rice, depending on the elevation of the farm parcel, and the season. Rice is the crop of choice because it is the very essence of the Korean farming tradition. It is the crop that will always bring a reasonable price, can always be sold, and is always useful in the farmer's household in all seasons.

The rice landscape for such an economic scene is most often terraced with the fields being edged by small mud walls. Water will be guided into the these fields as the rice seedlings are trans-planted from their nursery beds sometime in April or May—unless the farmer's crop land has been planted with winter wheat the prior September or October. If the June harvest of the wheat has been accomplished, the fields will be worked so that the wheat roots of the crop just harvested will be plowed under and mixed with the soil, cut up by the plow blades, and returned to raw plant material for the enrichment of the soil.

Water is let run on the fields so that it stands 3 to 5 inches (8 to 13 centimeters) deep before rice seedlings are transplanted into new fields. Seedlings that have been raised in small, intensely fertilized rice beds until they are 5 to 8 inches (13 to 20 centimeters) high are then brought to these paddy fields and planted in the wet soil in straight rows.

This pattern of farming has long involved many family members. The management of the irrigation waters and the transplanting of these new plants into the mushy soil of the beds set aside for the sunny summer rice season was a major task. The cultivation of this mother plant of the Korean farming economy was central to all the tasks largely handled by the small farming family.

Not only does the household economy relate closely to the tasks and outcome of this growing of rice (and perhaps winter wheat, soybeans, vegetables, and still other cash crops), but the household culture is also intricately linked with the cropping importance of rice. There is no other crop that means as much to the social as well as economic well being of a South Korean farming family as raising traditional rice.

The most simple of these households will have little farming machinery, but the more prosperous rural households will have small mechanized cultivators to assist in the field preparation and cultivation of rice and other crops.

The expanding importance of such mechanization—and it is more rapidly becoming part of the regular lowland farming images—has also had an influence on migration patterns in South Korea. As farm mechanization increases, there is a relative decline in the need for farm labor. Such a shift begins to push young Koreans away from the farming tradition and turn their heads toward the growing cities in South Korea— especially Seoul. South Korea has now become more than 80 percent urban (from less than one-third the percentage of just 40 years ago). This steady increase in urban ratios derives in good part from the decreasing capacity of family farms to meet both the economic and the social needs of Korean youth.

Realize that this South Korean farming world was, during

Small family-run farms still exist in the countryside. This woman works in the rice paddies and maintains the traditions of generations of peasant farmers.

the long period of Japanese colonization from 1910 until 1945, the "rice bowl" not only for Japan, but for the less productive lands of North Korea. Although the countryside is now losing youth steadily to urban futures, there is a long tradition of productive small-holder peasant farming in South Korea.

So, in thinking of the seven guidelines noted previously about economic development, it is clear that in the small farmer's world, there is attention to points 1 (work ethic) and 4 (live sparingly). There is also the use of opportunities for education, but it is not as available there as it is in the cities. In the scale of economic geography that is the Korean family farm, there is a great deal of self-sufficiency, family interdependence, and always the potential for some of the youth to leave the farm and head for the city in search of a different future.

This landscape and these scenes account for only 10 percent of the Korean population, but it is exactly this tradition that has been at the very center of this country's social and economic growth for not just decades, but for centuries.

The urban household

The parallel home unit to the small family farm in the Korean countryside is the crowded family household in any one of the growing cities in South Korea. Seoul is the most extreme case (with approximately 10 milllion people in the metropolitan area), but there are many cities in the industrial corridor running between Inchon and Seoul on the west central side of the peninsula. These cities have to absorb hundreds, even thousands, of new migrants monthly as the combination of the lure of the city and the only modest potential for economic prosperity in the countryside propel rural-to-urban migration streams.

In the South Korean city there is a world of modest apartments and rooms that are home to small families and sometimes not-so-small families. In the traditional economic situation, there would be (most often in the countryside and not in the city) two or even three generations living under one roof. The son would have his father and mother and perhaps his grandparents all living together. This extended family had an economic role to play, for it afforded some help with child care for the son (and his wife) as they tried to earn enough money to support this extended household.

In the countryside this pattern was somewhat easier, because there were more often productive rural chores that could occupy the time and utilize the skills of the senior members of the household. In the countryside, it was also much cheaper to get space for such a family. In the cities of today's South Korea, however, there is a premium to be paid for urban residential space, therefore large families tend to live in crowded accommodations—or, increasingly, they tend not to occur.

The urban household economy for a lower class or lower middle-class family in South Korea will have one or two wage earners in urban offices or retail stores. They may also have a child in higher education. All of the children in the age range of elementary and secondary schooling will be in school. There is a keen pride in South Korea in attaining education.

The people in this setting are always attentive to economic opportunities that might appear in the city setting. Often the young migrants who leave their rural beginnings and come to the city have little knowledge about how to find a job or to establish themselves so that they may start a family. However, the city (and this is true all through East Asia and through much of the world) seems rich in images of possible opportunity for people with ambition and energy.

In terms of the seven guidelines, this life setting uses 1 (work ethic), 2 (strive for education), 4 (live sparingly), and 6 (be good hosts to foreign enterprises or foreign guests— who might provide unexpected economic opportunity.) Think of this population as an approximate 20 to 30 percent of the urban economic livelihood in South Korean cities.

The government worker

A third small-scale example of economic pattern in South Korea is one associated with government employees. Such people also live in the city, they more often have not just migrated from the countryside, and they have taken full advantage of any educational opportunities available to them. They will live in modest apartments, often with their own family, but somewhat less often with several generations living in the same apartment. In having a longer history as a part of the city world, they have grown farther away from the economic and social traditions that were central to life in the past, to life in the rural sector of South Korea.

Working within the governmental framework means that they are likely to have somewhat more interaction with foreign influences. Their whole life outlook is more fully influenced by foreign movies, magazines, and television. Although a government employee does not earn a high salary, there is the potential for developing some arrangement with big business or a major project. Like so many whose economic lives are lived out in the cities of South Korea, there is more often the hope that some door might open that would lead to a more prosperous and exciting life. Failing to find that door, the urban governmental worker has a fairly stable and predictable existence.

In terms of the seven guidelines, the most significant factors are 2 (education), 3 (provide good opportunities for well-trained young people), 4 (live sparingly), 6 (be good hosts to foreign enterprises—and personnel), and 7 (seek out world markets—or at least foreign opportunities.) The government workers total about 15 percent of the urban work force, but the importance of this economic role is made even more significant by the fact that the authority held in such a role can be of considerable importance in the undertaking of major projects.

The businessman

At the heart of the South Korean economy for the past four decades has been the businessman. Looking at the last of these smaller-scale examples of how the South Korean economic landscape is shaped shows the following. Recalling that more than 80 percent of the Korean population currently lives in cities, there has to be a source for food, services, public order, and all those things that have to be provided to keep a city working at the neighborhood level. In the Korean city there would be a world of small markets that sold vegetables, fowl and fish, flowers, hats, gloves and umbrellas, undershirts, and rubber work shoes.

Businesspeople work hard to promote their goods and services. These marketplaces provide a firm beginning for families seeking to establish a life in the city.

These markets are like those markets that exist in the densely settled inner margins of American cities. A husband and wife and their older children (at least after school hours and on weekends) would be behind the counters and stocking the shelves. Such markets might be the product of a cooperative venture of a number of family members who want to become involved in the growing business realm of the city scene. Long hours, an uncertain future, and only modest return might characterize this South Korean businessman, but an investment, a store name, and a business tradition are all being developed around such an operation.

Children, uncles and aunts, and even grandparents might all be involved in the businessman's effort. The lessons learned in these narrow aisles, in the interaction with local police and even rowdy youth, and in working within the always demanding framework of municipal and provincial governmental rules and authority figures, all serve as vital education in preparing the Korean for potentially upgrading into larger business ventures. The sequence may finally lead to salaried jobs with the really big *chaebol* (the mega-corporations that grew out of traditional industrial family associations) that gave direction to the major Korean economic development since World War II. This growth built was on cooperative and competitive history that went back for decades or longer.

This small-scale family business scene utilizes the seven guidelines. The businesses strongly represent 1 (work ethic), 2 (education—demanding that their children do well in school even if it means losing good market labor in their shop), 3 (provide working opportunities for young people), 4 (live sparingly), and 6 (be good hosts—possibly to foreigners who might provide economic opportunities to some member of the family business).

As far as how representative the small business or businessman's family is of the urban population in South Korea, approximately 20–30 percent of the employed urban population is deeply engaged in independent economic activity. They help to sustain the continually expanding urban population in South Korea.

CHANGING THE SCALE IN ECONOMIC ASSESSMENT

The more local images of the small farm operation, the wage earner, the government employee, and the urban businessman are the underpinning of the demographic reality of South Korea. However, the dramatic successes that the country has had in the past four decades in the drama of evolving from a less-developed country to a major economic force in East Asia and beyond derives from a very different kind of economic scale. The dramatic elements of that process are the envy of many nations—both within and well beyond East Asia.

In giving data on the macroeconomic changes in the economic geography of South Korea within the past several decades, six items have been selected. They will give focus to the enormous success South Korea has realized in what it has accomplished since the end of the Korean War in 1953. South Korea is described as one of the four East Asian "dragons" (or "tigers") because of its economic performance and steady economic growth. The lessons learned from Korean development and general success can be utilized in looking at other developing nations as well.

The six factors are:

1. Imports. What value in U.S. dollars, and the two major items imported.
2. Export. What value in U.S. dollars, and the two major items exported.
3. Tourism income. The value in U.S. dollars of money brought to the country through tourism. This also becomes an index of political stability.
4. Household size. The number of people of all ages in an average household in South Korea.
5. Household income per year. This is the amount of money in U.S. dollars earned per year by all of the working members of the household. This does not include the cash value of things raised by the average household and consumed at home.
6. Gross national product (GNP). This is the total value of all goods and services produced by a country during a year, and it includes the gross domestic product (GDP) and the money earned from abroad. GNP is always larger than GDP.

The combination of these six factors will provide a good foundation for understanding the basis for the current economic geography and its general health in South Korea.

The dynamic that is more often considered in doing an assessment of a country's efforts to climb out of the category of "undeveloped (or sometimes less-developed) nations" and into the realm of "emerging nations" or—most desired— "more-developed nations" is the pattern of major trade conditions. The interrelationship of what a country imports, what it exports, and how much money it makes in that process is of dominant significance in economic growth.

South Korea has been conscious of this since the end of the Korean War and, especially in the past three decades, has given major resources, energy, and commitment to exactly these dimensions of economic change.

Consider the processes associated with the table below:

	Imports	Exports	Tourism Income	Household Size	Household Income/year	GNP
MACRO SCALE ECONOMIC INDICATORS IN SOUTH KOREAN DEVELOPMENT						
1962	$422 million	$55 million	NA	5.5	$420	xx
1985	$30.6 billion machinery & fuel 55% (of total)	$29.2 billion manufactured goods & machinery 87% of total	$596.2 million	4.5	$4,100	$78.9 billion
1992	$81.5 billion machinery & manufacturing 50% of total	$71.8 billion machinery & manufacturing 64%	$3.6 billion	3.8	$19,800	$231.1 billion
2001	$160.4 billion electronics & fuel 43% of total	$172.3 billion electronics & machinery 52% of total	$6.8 billion	3.6	$47,769	$397.9 billion

Encyclopedia Britannica Book of the Year, 1986, 1993, 2002; CIA World Factbook, 2002; Facts About Korea, 1984.

To make good use of a table like the one above, it is necessary to think of the factors that lead to successful economic development. The importance of imports is that it shows that the population is getting accustomed to items as small as toasters to things as large as major construction machinery. The South Korean government allowed importing, but it also put heavy taxes (tariffs) on consumer goods such as televisions and automobiles in the hope that the Korean interest in such goods would stimulate domestic investment and the development of factories.

In 1962 total imports amounted to $422 million while exports came to $55 million. By 1985 imports still exceeded exports because the South Korean economy had not yet developed enough strength to be a more commanding presence in global trade. However, imports ($30.6 billion) and exports ($29.2 billion) were both much better developed than in that first decade following the Korean War. The South Korean economy was beginning to develop a bold head of steam and ready to become much more significant in terms of broad-based economic development.

Although 1985 still had South Korea in a trade deficit (imports exceeded exports) there was a more reasonable balance with imports, even with the trade deficit. The goods that the country exported were primarily industrial machinery and manufactured goods. By that year, South Korea had become the world's 10th largest producer of steel. Most of this steel came from the Pohong Iron and Steel Company, which was located in a major industrial center near Seoul. By 1984, South Korea had also already begun to export automobiles (52,000 units in 1984) and was producing a total of 260,000 units altogether. This serves as a useful index of the increasingly industrial economic base being created in the country.

Tourist income is a good indicator of economic development because one of the patterns that has been so constant in the economic change that has been experienced in South Korea is the shift in the labor sector. The service sector (providing jobs for 68 percent of employed South Koreans in 2000) has been growing steadily. One of the catalysts for such growth is the tourist trade. Amounting to only a little more than

Manufacturing has increased since the end of the war. Cars manufactured in South Korea are exported to the United States and Western Europe and are recognized for their performance and affordability.

$500 million in the early 1980s, such trade and income grew to nearly $7 billion by 2001.

Household size is also an essential factor to understand when considering the dynamics of economic growth and economic geography. In 1962 the South Korean household size was above 5.5 people per family on average. By 1985 household size had dropped to 4.5 people per family. This still reflected a population growth rate of approximately 2 percent annually.

This means that all economic growth that took place would be, in essence, consumed by a doubling of the population in two to three decades. Every government that attempts to stimulate major economic growth and change has to pay major attention to the natural growth rate of its country's population.

Household income per year is another way to look at the levels of cash available for home consumption, and also as potential savings for domestic industrial development. In 1962, South Korea had a per capita income of $82. In 1985 the index in South Korea (but for the full household) was $4,100.

The final index to use with this table is the gross national product (GNP). This is the total value of all goods (including agricultural and industrial goods) and services. In 1985 South Korea had brought its level of productivity to nearly $80 billion in value, up from less than $2 billion 15 years earlier.

By 1985 all of these index numbers had changed remarkably. Imports and exports had grown to $30.6 billion and $29.2 billion, respectively. Although there was still more import trade than export trade, the national economy had reached a close balance. Tourism amounted to just under $600 million. Household size had diminished to 4.5 people on average. By this time, too, South Korea had shown enough clear potential for growth and organization to win the site for the 1988 Olympic Games. They were to be held in Seoul, the national capital.

In household income, the growth between 1962 and 1985 was dramatic. Coming from a base of less than $500 per household in the decade following the end of the Korean War (1950–1953), family income rose to $4,100 per year. This level of prosperity took South Korea beyond the income level of Taiwan, way beyond that of the People's Republic of China, and the rest of the countries in Southeast Asia (with the exception of the urban unit of Singapore, and the then-British colony of Hong Kong).

The country's GNP in 1985 had climbed to $78.9 billion. This came about—as did much of the rest of the rapid economic development in the 1960s and 1970s—because of a series of Five Year Plans conceived by the government. These strategic development plans set in motion very specific programs in industrial and transportation development. South Korea has prided itself in working within the general context of capitalism and democracy. Yet much of the economic change that characterized these two decades between the 1962 first Five Year Plan and the middle 1980s was shaped exactly by government planners as they worked with the country's largest industrial conglomerates. There was minimal investment in light industrial consumer goods for local consumption and much more of a focus on turning out goods for export.

The Indices in 1992 and 2001

Although imports doubled between 1992 and 2001 ($81.5 billion to $160.4 billion), exports increased even more ($71.8 billion to $172.3 billion) so that the South Korean economy did very well. This was a particularly difficult time because of the so-called Asian Flu of 1997–1999. That "flu" relates to an economic turndown that swept across East Asia and Southeast Asia in late 1997 and brought almost all national economies to a critical stand-still by early 1998. South Korea, in handling that crisis, showed itself to be a very strong economy. It was able to secure a loan of $57 billion in 1998 and through the use of that money was able to liquidate many of the weakest links in the national economy.

Almost more amazing than the government's success in making sound fiscal policy come from the distribution of the International Monetary Fund (IMF) loan in 1998, was the government's actual and timely repayment of that massive loan. It was in the middle of 2001 that the government announced that the full $57 billion had been repaid and that economic growth in South Korea was again on the positive side of the ledger. Actually, South Korea had hardly ever gone negative in its annual growth, but its pace had dropped from the 9 to 13 percent range into a low 3 to 5 percent range.

Among the sites to visit is the Haein-sa (which means "reflection on a calm sea") monastery, which is used by Chogye monks of the Zen school of Buddhism. The monastery complex houses Buddhist texts carved on wooden blocks.

As is shown in the table's tourism index, tourism grew from $3.6 billion in 1992 to $6.8 billion 2001. Some of this was still tied to the enormous success South Korea had had in its hosting of the 1988 Olympics. The country also continued to play a role for regional international sports competitions, such as the World Soccer Cup in the middle of 2002.

The growth of tourism also relates again to the seven guidelines that were presented earlier. Recall that guideline 6 said "be good hosts to foreign enterprises" and 7 was "seek out world markets." Point 6 had been quite evident in the 1988 games, and the big increase in foreign tourism overall gave the South Koreans ever more opportunity to show off the impressive economic growth of their country.

Finally, by 2001 household size had dropped to an average of 3.6 people, and household income had risen to $47,769. The national GNP was $397.9 billion in 2001. In terms of what is called gross national product purchasing power parity (GNP PPP) South Korea had reached $16,100 per person by 2000. This compares to $24,900 for Japan; $26,500 for Singapore; $2,200 for India; and $3,600 for China for the same year. North Korea in 2001 had a GNP PPP of $1,000.

In the classic sense of economic geography, South Korea has a thin natural resource base. It does possess some iron ore. It has been the base for a rapidly developing steel industry. Some iron ore is also exported to Japan. Tungsten is an important metal in the manufacture of specialty steels, lighting filaments, and some electronics goods. It is a resource that South Korea possesses enough of to supply some as export to the United States and also support its intricate steel industry.

The country also has a low-grade anthracite coal and, as noted earlier, some hydroelectric capacity. Coal is a frustrating resource because it was so vital at the outset of the Industrial Revolution two and a half centuries ago, but now is seen as a negative fuel source because of its heavy contribution to smog and greenhouse gases.

There is only a small petroleum base in South Korea. The thermal power (coal-fueled) stations have been slowly and steadily converted to fuel oil-fired stations, but this transition has come at a high cost. The country must import so much of its petroleum that is at the center of the country's steadily expanding industrial economy.

The real resource that has made a difference in South Korea for a long time is the country's capacity to raise rice and other foods. In comparisons between the south and north regions of the Korean Peninsula, it is the south that is the breadbasket. A country that can develop agricultural self-sufficiency as South Korea has done also gains the confidence to expand into new industrial activities. South Korea has done well with its resource base. South Korea came out of World War II and then the Korean Conflict just barely able to sustain its population, and it is now a country that ranks in the top dozen of the world's industrial powers.

The resource most impressive in the economic record of South Korea, however, is the human resource. It is because of the country's capacity to educate, to save, and to limit economic focus to export markets in the 1960s, 1970s, and part of the 1980s that it became such an economic power. Recall that virtually all of the East Asian economies fell into deep negative slides during the 1997 "Asian Flu" period of failing economies, but South Korea was the first one to climb out of negative growth and regain strong positive growth. In 2002, South Korea had the third highest gross domestic product growth rate (5.7 percent vs. 7.6 percent for China and 7.5 percent for Peru) of the so-called emerging markets.

South Korea is a country that has made enormous progress in the use of a meager resource base. It has done so through a continued agricultural and industrial productivity because of the brilliant (and sometimes overly demanding) utilization of its best resource—its human energy, skill, and dedication.

Seoul is a city of newly built high-rise apartment buildings and older low-rise buildings. The area has a population of over 10 million and is the center of government, education, entertainment, and business

7

Contemporary South Korean Regional Identities

T his chapter focuses on people, places, and some very specific landscapes in South Korea. These specific images also stand as good representations of similar settings around the country. The first is the capital city, Seoul, located in the northwest corner of the country on the important Han River.

SEOUL

Seoul is a Korean term that means "capital city," and it has been the single most important city in South Korea from the beginning of the divided peninsula's two-country pattern. Seoul is currently not only the administrative head of the country, it is also the center of South Korean commercial, industrial, and cultural activities. It is a true primate city—which means that it is twice as large as the next biggest city, and it is the leading urban center in virtually all of the cultural and economic developments in the country. Paris, France, is a good example of another primate city.

In 1392, at the beginning of the Yi dynasty (or Choson dynasty), the Korean city of Hansong (now Seoul) was a classic oriental city of Chinese design. It was a walled city with four main gates and four secondary gates. The walls were oriented in cardinal directions so that there was an explicit north, south, west, and east gate. These four main gates had secondary gates in the walls as well. There are still two of those early gates that exist in modern form. Such city design was a direct expression of the importance of Chinese cultural traits and their diffusion into the Korean Peninsula. Hansong was made the capital of the Choson dynasty in 1394 and played that role until the 1910 annexation of the Korean Peninsula by the Japanese.

The city site is significant because it is on the Han River, which flows from the mountains in the north and east down across the breadth of the peninsula and then pours into the Yellow Sea north of another major industrial city, Inchon. The corridor that lies between Seoul and Inchon has become steadily more industrialized and densely settled. This whole area is approximately 25–30 miles (40–48 kilometers) south of the border between North and South Korea.

During the Korean War (1950–1953), the city of Seoul was captured and retaken by South Korean and North Korean forces four different times. Each time, more of the city was destroyed through artillery fire and warfare. Even with the beginning of the first skyscrapers in the early 1970s, growth of a major urban skyline has been erratic as the country has been buffeted by economic down times (the worst of which was the late 1990s).

Seoul, in its broadest metropolitan range, has a population

of approximately 10 to 11 million now, or nearly one-quarter of the population of the entire country lives in this urban center. It has an urban density of approximately 60,000 people per square mile (23,160 per square kilometer). (Manhattan has approximately 26,000 per square mile [10,036 per square kilometer].) As important as it is in so many economic ways, it is even more powerful as a magnet for the steadily increasing flow of rural youth to urban places. Seoul is the prime center for the sense of opportunity, as a source of stories (and not all good) about the experiences other country folk have had in making their shift from the rural life to the city. Seoul is the representation of the profound difference in life that could occur if the migrant happened to get a factory job, happened to find a place to live (perhaps with someone from the same rural area), or happened to get involved in something that provided a different scenario than rural tradition and marginal poverty.

More than half of Seoul's 1.7 million households are in apartment buildings. The idea of a multistory building beyond three stories was nearly unknown until recently. Such a shift in urban landscape is not remarkable in a global sense, but in giving South Koreans a new world to see and live in, such a change is greatly significant.

Seoul is also the educational center of the country. More than 50 universities and colleges are in Seoul—or more than one-quarter of all the educational institutions in South Korea. Such a preponderance of educational centrality is another proof of the primate city status of this city. It also has the major share of the museums, theaters, and recreation places in the country.

In the successful 1988 Summer Olympic Games hosted by South Korea, most of the recreational facilities were in—or at the edge of—Seoul. Still part of the landscape are the Olympic stadium, gymnasium, indoor pool, baseball

The Summer Olympic Games were held in Seoul from September 17 to October 2, 1988. Hosting the games provided the opportunity for Koreans to highlight the achievements made in the city in the years following the Korean war.

stadium, and a number of smaller athletic venues. There is also an Olympic Park east of the major stadium, and it has the classic Mongch'on Fortress of early Seoul at its center.

In terms of landscape imagery, Seoul is a great reflection of the close proximity of the old and the new in urban space. New skyscrapers are close to 70-year-old small buildings that still reflect the smaller town origins of this place. Sophisticated businesspeople in Western clothes can be seen walking down wide commercial streets lined with restaurants from European as well as Asian traditions. People in simple farming garb are likely to be on these streets as well, looking dumbfounded as they peer up at the height of buildings that they have not even dreamed possible.

This city is the city of the future that many Koreans thought could never be achieved. There is enormous national pride in the fact that it has been achieved, and has been achieved primarily by national effort.

THE DEMILITARIZED ZONE

One of the most identifiable landscapes of the Korean Peninsula is the deadly, highly land-mined strip of land that separates these two parts of what has historically been a single nation. The images of this demilitarized zone (DMZ) have been captured effectively in this short essay by Cathy Salter that appeared in the *Columbia Tribune,* a local newspaper. Read it and think of what these images signify.

From a Distance: Korean Reconciliation?

In the chill of an early summer dawn, I watch four geese glide on steam rising off the surface of our pond. The scene looks frozen and eerily distant, as timeless as cranes on an ancient Korean scroll. From our summer porch, I watch them reach the bank and walk toward the barn. A cup of coffee and steamed milk warms my hands. It is now officially summer, but the scene and cool morning air have reminded me of a distant country frozen for half a century in a cold war of isolation and deeply divisive hostility.

From a distance the fog-shrouded bank around the

pond could be a snowy hillside somewhere in North or South Korea. Winter is a season this divided country knows well. In impoverished and isolated North Korea, a feudal place tottering on the brink of collapse, winters can be brutal. By the late 1990s, years of failed crops had brought famine and trees had been stripped for food and fuel. From afar, photojournalists presented the world with starkly contrasting images of the two Koreas as the last century came to a close.

Malnourished North Korean children critically ill with pneumonia were photographed being sent home from hospitals because there was no fuel for heat. Images of South Korea were of a democratic, technologically developed, internationally connected, open market society.

World powers concerned about stability in East Asia seem to agree on the need for reconciliation of South and North Korea, divided along the 38th parallel for much of my lifetime. Almost half a century after its creation, the DMZ—a 151-mile-long, 2.5-mile-wide demilitarized border zone dividing the two Koreas—is an empty quarter of mines, barbed wire, tank traps, and underground tunnels. In the absence of human activity, the strip has become a refuge for the Manchurian crane—ironically, the bird of peace in some Asian cultures.

From a distance, I look out on the beauty of Breakfast Creek [Missouri], green from recent summer rains, and try to imagine peace in such an unnaturally vacant place. On either side of this no-man's land, the world's largest concentration of hostile troops maintain a tense vigil that began when an armistice was arranged following the 1950–53 Korean War. Almost half a century later, the United States still maintains approximately 37,000 service personnel in South Korea who support and coordinate operations with the 650,000-strong Korean armed forces.

This month, as the first summer of the new century is

preparing to heat up in the Midwest, the world's attention has been focused on a photograph of Korea's two leaders—Kim Dae Jung, the South's president, and Kim Jong Il, the North's reclusive leader—taken at an historic summit in Pyongyang, North Korea's capital. They are standing side by side, hands clasped overhead, having just toasted the signing of a joint declaration to work toward eventual reunification of their two countries—technically at war for nearly half a century.

In 1987, I took several of my 9th grade students to hear then-exiled, former political prisoner Kim Dae Jung speak at a World Affairs Council luncheon in Los Angeles. Kim spoke of the need for political liberalization in South Korea, including greater freedom of the press, greater freedoms of expression and assembly, and the restoration of the civil rights of former detainees. A decade later, this courageous man who narrowly escaped assassination and execution on several occasions became South Korea's president in the country's first true opposition party victory in a presidential election.

Since his election, Kim Dae Jung has articulated an engagement policy toward the North. This month, he arrived at the inter-Korean summit with offers of investment and major infrastructure projects in an effort to help the North repair its shattered economy. From a distance, the two Korean leaders appear to be moving with both optimism and caution, beginning first with talk of trade and family contacts. There is hope that in the coming months, families separated since the Korean War will be reunited. Political and military issues including the withdrawal of American troops from South Korea and the North's nuclear ambitions and long-range missile arsenals—two security issues of great concern to America, Japan, Russia, and China—will take more time and require lengthy negotiation.

Perhaps in the coming decade, reforms and democratization will find their way into North Korea, and the vast empty corridor that now divides the two Koreas at the 38th parallel will have become a permanent wildlife sanctuary for the Manchurian crane. What is now an ugly scar on the landscape could in time become a place for reconciliation and healing—a quiet reminder of just how far these two countries will have come in their mine-filled journey toward peace.

This landscape of separation is a ribbon of uncertainty. It is one of the most heavily land-mined pieces of land in the world today. Both the South and North Korean armies have a continual fear of the enemy (sometimes relatives, as in the American Civil War) sneaking across the DMZ. It was this zone that the North Koreans crossed in force in June 1950 in an effort to reunite the two halves of the Korean Peninsula under the power of their red flag. For three years there was bloody warfare north of, south of, and across this strip.

In April 1996 the North Koreans came across the line again in an effort to redress some attack or spying of which they accused the South Koreans. Even with the continuing efforts of President Kim Dae Jung (noted in the essay above) there has been no genuine shift in the approach to changing the policy toward this zone. Recently, in the summer of 2002, there was the sinking of a South Korean vessel in the waters off Inchon with the death of 4 South Korean sailors and some 30 North Koreans killed by the return gunfire. These incidents not only keep the DMZ very much a tense landscape between the two adversaries, but they also make the larger political moves that have been made in attempting to open the doors between North and South Korea—and the United States—virtually meaningless.

The South Korean soldiers patrol near a barbed-wire fence in the demilitarized zone (DMZ) in April 1996 after North Korean soldiers marched into the zone.

Think about an arbitrary line drawn across the map of a peninsula jutting out from the continent of Asia. The line becomes a political separation in 1945. It becomes a military objective in 1950. In 2002, it now stands as an avenue of hatred and danger separating two halves of a country that had known varying degrees of independence for more than two millennia.

CHEJU DO

The island of Cheju (Cheju do) at the southern tip of the Korean Peninsula has a long history of its own traditions. Unlike the larger island of Tsushima that lies further east and slightly north of Cheju do, this island has been clearly Korean territory from the beginning of Korean political identity. It has been known in the West as Quelpart Island.

It bears many of the same landscapes as South Korea—that is, grain, soybeans, sweet potatoes, and cotton are raised—but fishing is very important and villages, more than large cities, are the most common settlements. It is approximately 700 square miles (1,813 square kilometers) in size and has a population of just over 500,000 people, with more than half of them living in Cheju City, the port city nearest the peninsula.

However, Cheju Island has the special history of being the locale where the Mongol leader, Kublai Khan, stopped in 1272–1273 in his effort to invade Japan. The Mongol leader had his men (men who were familiar with neither sailing nor farming generally) build vessels that they would use in 1273 to make their attempt to sail across the East China Sea into the Sea of Japan to attack the west side of Honshu, Japan's largest island. Cheju was the staging point for this powerful horse-riding army that had been marching both east and west across the northern plains of Inner Asia.

The attack failed. It failed because the floating Mongols and their Korean crews were faced with a typhoon of such magnitude that few or no ships made it to Japan, and many were not able to return to Cheju Do. This was not the only attempt made by the Mongols to extend the power of their unprecedentedly extensive land kingdom to the islands of Japan, but it was the one that has a place of lore in the tradition of Cheju.

Kim Jong Il (left), North Korea's president, and Kim Dae Jung, South Korea's president, met in the North Korea capital of Pyongyang in 2000 to discuss the state of affairs between the two countries on the divided peninsula.

The Future of South Korea

T he future of South Korea pivots on generally the same variables as that of other nations caught up in the demanding and ambitious efforts of economic growth. In the eyes of many, the South Korean future should be more secure than that of parallel nations, because the growth and development patterns established in the past three decades have been so strong. This view is supported particularly because South Korea did such an impressive job in the timely repayment of the $57 billion loan that the International Monetary Fund provided in 1997–1998.

However, things are not that simple. South Korea has to deal with the specter of the presence of one of the world's largest standing armies just north of the 38th parallel, continually claiming South Korean injustices and provocations. Even though President Kim Dae Jung won the Nobel Peace Prize in 2000 because of his contributions to "democracy and human rights in South Korea and East Asia in general, and for peace and reconciliation with North Korea in particular," he still is a great distance from success in this effort.

In 2000, President Kim of South Korea initiated a meeting with North Korean leader Kim Jong Il to be held in Pyongyang, North Korea. This was the first summit meeting of these two leaders who discussed such matters as family reunification and possible reduction of on-going tensions between the two Korean countries. There was talk of a package of economic benefits as well.

South Korea agreed to launch car-building facilities in the north (producing, among other units, Fiat and Alfa Romeo subcompacts). The largest component of this new cooperation came in the development of a major tourism program funded by the Hyundai Group, one of the largest auto manufacturing operations in South Korea. Hyundai plans to spend more than $900 million in a five-year period for tourism development. Hyundai is putting great stock in this potential, for in 1998–1999, more than 180,000 South Koreans (and a few foreigners) visited Mount Kumkang just north of the DMZ.

Much of this solid beginning was called into question in 2002 when North Korea killed four South Korean sailors in a battle between the two sides on the west side of the peninsula, near the western edge of the DMZ. Thus this particular landscape continues to be a place of tension.

Beyond the political uncertainty of the divided peninsula, South Korea also has an increasingly strident urban work force. For nearly three decades, Korean laborers who have been the backbone of steel, auto, machinery, and textile industries have worked with minimal benefits and voice. Yet they have been the major contributors to the dramatic processes that have put the South Korean economy in the top dozen of global producers. Conditions are now changing as unions begin to take shape and make demands on the *chaebol* (the traditional corporate conglomerates that run the country's largest business operations).

Laser lights illuminate an enormous soccer ball that was erected in front of Seoul's city hall to celebrate the World Cup soccer games, which were hosted by South Korea and Japan in 2002.

South Korea's cohosting (with Japan) of the 2002 World Cup soccer series (in which the South Korean team beat Poland but got no farther in the intense competition) provided the country a major opportunity to demonstrate its economic strength. Ten stadiums were either constructed or reconstructed in order to accommodate this spirited competition. In the fall of 2002, South Korea expanded the use of these new facilities and hosted the Asian Games. In these competitions, there was not only the opportunity for showcasing the country's new economic and sports prowess, but the opening ceremonies provided an event that had the South Korean and North Korean teams entering the Games marching under a single white flag showing the Korean peninsula in a single, solid color.

In December of that year, lawyer Roh Moo-hyun was elected president. The South Korean constitution disallowed

President Kim Dae Jung from running again. The election of Roh is seen as a symbol of the country's development of a stable democratic system. Roh came to power on a wave of anti-American protests, stimulated in part by popular demands for expanded interaction with North Korea. President Kim Dae Jung had initiated the first face-to-face talks with North Korean president Kim Jung-Il in 2000 and it was expected that President Roh would continue to promote the process of political and social thawing between the two Koreas. This put the new president in a very awkward position since the Bush administration in the United States was turning ever more harsh in its attitudes toward North Korea.

In 2004, after a year of declining economic growth in South Korea, President Roh made the mistake of making a public declaration in support of the Uri Party, the party that had supported his presidential candidacy a year earlier. President Roh was consequently impeached. A stipulation in the South Korean constitution disallows a sitting president from promoting his own party. Roh challenged the South Korean parliament to impeach him. In May 2004, the South Korean Constitutional Court ruled against impeachment and Roh anticipated four more years of presidency.

South Korea sent 3,000 troops to Iraq in support of the U.S.-led war against Saddam Hussein. In June 2004, a hostage-taking group calling for the withdrawal of all Korean troops from Iraq beheaded a young Korean. Roh refused to withdraw the troops but claimed they were involved only in reconstruction projects and not actual combat. This gave even more fuel to the street protests over South Korean involvement in the Iraq war.

The tension in Seoul and South Korea also continued at a high level because of the difficulty of engineering any tangible and useful political or social exchange with North Korea. There was no relaxation of the enmity between the two Koreas. Roh's government is in a difficult place for it feels a keen sense of obligation to maintain reasonable relations with the Bush administration because of its ongoing consideration of the reduction of American armed forces in South Korea.

At the close of 2004, South Korea's economy was regaining some strength and there were more scheduled meetings of South Korea, Japan, North Korea, China, Russia, and the United States in Beijing. These six-nation meetings were powerfully significant in the future of South Korea because of the South Korean belief that they would be the first target that North Korea would select if Kim Jung-Il ever decided to demonstrate the military capacity that his standing army and alleged nuclear arms possessed.

Facts at a Glance

Geographic Coordinates	Kiev: 50° 27′ North, 30° 30′ East
Full country name	Taehan Min'guk (Republic of Korea)
Area	38,432 square miles (99,538 square kilometers)
Highest point	Halla-san (Mt. Halla) 6,398 feet (1,950 meters) above sea level
Population	47,925,000
People	99.9 percent Korean
Urban population	83 percent
Life expectancy	Male 71.5; Female 79.1
Capital	Seoul
Major cities	Seoul, Pusan, Taegu, Inchon, Taejon
Official language	Korean
Other language	English, Chinese
Religions	Christian, 48%; Buddhist, 47%; Confucian, 3%; other, 1%

Economy

Major products	Automobiles, ships, electronics, textiles
Gross national product	$447.6 billion
Economic sectors	Shipbuilding, electronics, motor vehicles
Currency	Won
Average annual income	$9,460 per capita

Government

Form of Government	Unitary multiparty republic with National Assembly
Voting rights	All citizens over 20 are allowed to vote
Political divisions	Provinces and five cities treated as provinces

108 B.C.	China conquers the northern half of Korean Peninsula.
313 A.D.	Korean forces drove the Chinese from Korea.
1259	Mongol armies conquered Korea.
1368	Koreans gained freedom from Mongol rule.
1392	The Yi dynasty was founded and lasted until 1910.
1590s	Japanese forces invaded Korea but were driven out by Korean armies.
1630s	Manchu armies invaded Korea from northern China and had powerful control in Korea but the Yi dynasty continued to serve as kings.
1642	Korea closed its borders to all nations except for an annual tribute ship from China. It became known as The Hermit Kingdom.
1876	Japan forced Korea to open its ports and begin wider foreign trade.
1910	Japanese annexed Korea.
1945	Soviet forces occupied northern Korea, and U.S. forces occupied southern Korea and this led to 1948 division of the peninsula into two countries.
1948	The Republic of Korea was created from the southern peninsula; the Democratic People's Republic of Korea was created from the northern.
1950–1953	The Korean War was a battle between the forces of North Korea and Chinese "volunteer" armies and the South Korean army and 17 UN member states' armies—mostly from the United States.
1988	South Korea hosted the Summer Olympic Games outside of Seoul.
1991	Talks between representatives of North and South Korea in effort to negotiate a reunification had some success in lowering tension levels between the two halves of the Korean Peninsula, but did little toward a reunification.

1992 Fuller political links with the People's Republic of China established.

2000 South Korean president Kim Dae Jung won the Nobel Peace Prize for work he had done in trying to bring North and South Korea closer.

2002 South Korea cohosted (with Japan) the world Soccer Cup in June and played single host to the Asian Games in the fall. Lawyer Roh Moo-hyun was elected president in December. He succeeded 2000 Nobel Peace Prize Laureate Kim Dae Jung as president.

2003 Roh Moo-hyun was inaugurated as president in February. As part of the country's continuing economic development, the Hyundai Shipyard became the largest ship building facility in the world. South Korea also became a global leader in both manufacture and use of electronic telecommunications devices.

2004 President Roh was impeached in March because of some comments he made in the promotion of his own political party (the Uri Party). However, in May the South Korean Constitutional Court ruled against the impeachment. There were also two meetings of the U.S., South Korea, Japan, Russia, North Korea and China in Beijing regarding North Korea's potential for the creation of atomic weapons.

Blaut, J. M. *The Colonizer's Model of the World.* New York: Guilford Press. 1993.

Cumings, Bruce. *Korea's Place in the Sun: A Modern History.* New York: W.W. Norton. 1997.

Duus, Peter. *The Abacus and the Sword: The Japanese Penetration of Korea, 1895–1910.* Berkeley: University of California Press. 1995

Kim, Elaine H., and Eui-Young Yu. *East to America: Korean American Life Stories.* New York: The New York Press. 1996.

Kolb, Albert. *East Asia China, Japan, Korea, Vietnam: Geography of a Cultural Region.* London: Methuen & Co. 1971.

Lautensach, Hermann. *Korea: A Geography Based on the Author's Travels and Literature.* Berlin: Springer-Verlag. 1988.

Lee, Kenneth B. *Korea and East Asia: The Story of a Phoenix.* Boulder, CO: Praeger Publishers, 1997.

McCune, Evelyn. *The Arts of Korea: An Illustrated History.* Rutland, VT: Tuttle. 1962.

Nilsen, Robert. Moon Handbooks: South Korea. Emeryville, CA: Avalon Travel Publishing. 1997.

Oberdorfer, Don. *The Two Koreas: A Contemporary History.* New York: Basic Books. 2001.

Phillips, Douglas A., and Steven C. Levi. *The Pacific Rim Region: Emerging Giant.* Hillside, NJ: Enslow Publishers. 1988

Storey, Robert and Eunkyong Park. *Korea.* Oakland, CA: Lonely Planet Publications. 2001.

Woronoff, Jon. *Korea's Economy: Man-Made Miracle.* Arch Cape, OR: Pace International Research, Inc. 1983.

Bibliography

Cressey, George B. *Asia's Lands and Peoples: A Geography of One-third of the Earth and Two-thirds of Its People.* New York: McGraw-Hill, 1963.

Encyclopedia Britannica *Book of the Year.* 1986-2002. Chicago: Encyclopedia Britannica, Inc.

Hoon, Shim Jae. "Summit Lifeline." *Far Eastern Economic Review.* April 20,2000. p. 44.

Kim, H. Edward, ed. *Facts About Korea.* Seoul, Korea: Hdlym Corporation, 1984.

Kolb, Albert. *East Asia China, Japan, Korea, Vietnam: Geography of a Cultural Region.* London: Methuen & Co, 1971.

Korea: Its Land, People, and Culture of All Ages. Seoul: Hakwon-sa Ltd, 1963.

Korean Overseas Information Services. *A Handbook of Korea.* New Jersey: Hdlym International Corporation. 1993.

Lee, Kenneth B. *Korea and East Asia: The Story of a Phoenix.* Boulder, CO: Praeger Publishers, 1997.

Reeve, W.D. *The Republic of Korea: A Political and Economic Study.* New York: Oxford University Press. 1963.

Reischauer, Edwin O. and John K. Fairbank. *East Asia: The Great Tradition.* Boston: Houghton Mifflin. 1960.

Salter, Cathy. "From a Distance: Korean Reconciliation?" Columbia, MO: *The Columbia Tribune.* June 28, 2000. p. 7A.

Salter, Christopher L. and Joseph J. Hobbs. *Essentials of World Regional Geography.* Pacific Grove, CA: Brooks/Cole Publishing, 2003.

Spencer, Joseph E. *Asia East by South.* New York: John Wiley & Sons, 1967.

"The Dead are Not the Only Casualties." *The Economist* July 6, 2002. p. 41.

Weightman, Barbara A. *Dragons and Tigers: A Geography of South, East, and Southeast Asia.* New York: John Wiley & Sons, 2002.

World Book Encyclopedia. Chicago: World Book, Inc., 2000.

Youn-Suk Kim and Kap-Soo Oh. *The US Korea Economic Partnership.* USA. Avebury, 1995.

Index

Index

page:

8:	Gail S. Ludwig	65:	AP/Wide World Photos
11:	21st Century Publishing	68:	AP/Wide World Photos
13:	AP/Wide World Photos	86:	AP/Wide World Photos
19:	21st Century Publishing	91:	Gail S. Ludwig
25:	© Bohemian Nomad Picturemakers/ Corbis	94:	© Bohemian Nomad Picturemakers/ Corbis
32:	© Bettmann/Corbis	98:	AP/Wide World Photos
37:	Gail S. Ludwig	103:	AP/Wide World Photos
45:	Gail S. Ludwig	106:	AP/Wide World Photos
50:	AP/Wide World Photos	109:	AP/Wide World Photos
56:	AP/Wide World Photos		

Frontis: Flag courtesy of *theodora.com/flags*. Used with permission.

Cover: © Chris Lisle/CORBIS

CHRISTOPHER L. "KIT" SALTER spent three years teaching English at a Chinese university and has traveled to East Asia eight different times across a period of nearly thirty years. He is a geographer who did his dissertation on a Chinese theme, but has taught about the larger world of East Asia for decades at UCLA and at the University of Missouri—Columbia. He has also been involved in geography education and has been awarded the National Geographic Society "Distinguished Geography Educator" Award (the first one ever given), and the "George Miller" Award from the National Council for Geographic Education. He lives on a small farmlet in central Missouri with his wife Cathy, who is a writer.

CHARLES F. "FRITZ" GRITZNER is Distinguished Professor of Geography at South Dakota University in Brookings. He is now in his fifth decade of college teaching and research. During his career, he has taught more than 60 different courses, spanning the fields of physical, cultural, and regional geography. In addition to his teaching, he enjoys writing, working with teachers, and sharing his love for geography with students. As consulting editor for the MODERN WORLD NATIONS series, he has a wonderful opportunity to combine each of these "hobbies." Fritz has served as both president and executive director of the National Council for Geographic Education and has received the Council's highest honor, the George J. Miller Award for Distinguished Service.